THE FASHION
CHRONICLES

The style stories of history's best dressed

THE FASHION CHRONICLES

CHRONICLES

The style stories of history's best dressed

Amber Butchart

MITCHELL BEAZLEY

For Rob and new beginnings

An Hachette UK Company
www.hachette.co.uk

First published in Great Britain in 2018 by Mitchell Beazley,
an imprint of
Octopus Publishing Group Ltd
Carmelite House
50 Victoria Embankment
London EC4Y 0DZ
www.octopusbooks.co.uk
www.octopusbooksusa.com

Distributed in the US by
Hachette Book Group
1290 Avenue of the Americas
4th and 5th Floors
New York, NY 10104

Distributed in Canada by
Canadian Manda Group
664 Annette St.
Toronto, Ontario, Canada M6S 2C8

ISBN 978 1 78472 381 1

A CIP catalogue record for this book is available from the British Library.

Printed and bound in China

10 9 8 7 6 5 4 3 2 1

Commissioning Editor Joe Cottington
Senior Editor Pauline Bache
Copy Editor Catherine Hooper
Art Director and Designer Yasia Williams-Leedham
Picture Research Manager Giulia Hetherington
Senior Production Controller Allison Gonsalves

Contents

Introduction

Costly thy habit as thy purse can buy,
But not express'd in fancy; rich, not gaudy;
For the apparel oft proclaims the man.

William Shakespeare, *Hamlet* (c.1599–1602),
Act I, Scene 3, Line 70.

From Eve's fig leaf to Hillary Clinton's pantsuit, the way we choose to adorn our bodies communicates myriad meanings. Across cultures and throughout history people have used clothing to signify power and status, to decorate and beautify, and to prop up (or dismantle) regimes and display political allegiances. As such, sartorial stories form the backdrop of history and, when uncovered, they can be illuminating, entertaining and informative. *The Fashion Chronicles* is a manifesto for dress history, illustrating how clothing intersects with culture, politics and art, and how the study of clothing can act as a portal to the past.

Scientific analysis estimates that modern humans were wearing clothing 170,000 years ago, corresponding with the onset of an ice age. It has even been suggested that clothing use was one of the technologies that enabled early populations to migrate out of Africa,[1] and that the adoption of clothing had repercussions on the development of modern human behaviour.[2] Clothing is central to the human experience, and prehistoric clothed bodies, such as the Nordic Egtved Girl and Alpine Ötzi the Iceman, are vital to our understanding of the past. Unlocking the secrets of their clothing tells us about migration, trade and the structure of societies.

Some of our most well-known historical figures were also the best dressed, their style resonating through the centuries to impact our wardrobes today. King Charles II of England and Beau Brummell hold esteemed places in the evolution of the man's suit, while the drapery of Ancient Greece, as captured in the poetry of Sappho, remains a design staple. Cleopatra and Boudicca were great leaders who have become iconic figures referenced on catwalks and movie screens. Controversial trendsetters, from Marie Antoinette and Georgiana Cavendish, Duchess of Devonshire to the Duke of Windsor, are lauded as style savants, while influential figures within the world of fashion defied the traditional to forge their own rules, such as magazine editor Diana Vreeland, designer Barbara Hulanicki and interior-designer-turned-muse Iris Apfel.

Historically, the power and wealth of the ruling class was displayed through dress: the 17th-century court finery of King Louis XIV of France, the coral beads of the Benin king, Oba Ewuare, and the luscious silks of Qianlong Emperor of China. A rise through the social ranks is a journey told in clothes, from Thomas Cromwell at the English Tudor court to the Italian Arnolfini merchants in 15th-century Bruges. Political allegiance can also be read on the body, whether fighting for women's rights in the case of Amelia Bloomer, Chimamanda Ngozi Adichie and Dame Christabel Pankhurst, or running for government like socialist Keir Hardie. Dress chimes with revolutionary ideals, as seen in Jacques Hébert's *sans-culottes* and Che Guevara's battle fatigues and beret.

National and cultural identity is encoded and expressed through dress. An affiliation with adopted countries was forged in the wardrobes of Queen Amalia of Greece, Queen Marie of Romania and Catherine the Great of Russia. Garments tell the story of an empire or nation, from the statesmanlike toga of Emperor Augustus to the tartans of Sir Walter Scott. Clothing also documents a transitional time in a nation's history, from ensuing globalization in the case of Empress Myeongseong of Korea, to national independence in India, a story told in the homespun cotton of Jawaharlal Nehru, the country's first Prime Minister. Genghis Khan's Silk Road, Shah Jahan's chintz and Yinka Shonibare's Dutch wax fabric show how textiles have shaped the world in which we live today.

The evolution of sportswear and shifting ideas around the public display of the body are tracked in Annette Kellerman's swimwear, Suzanne Lenglen's tennis garb, Jules Léotard's *maillot* and the athleisure of Beyoncé. The stage has always been a site of spectacular style, from Vesta Tilley in Victorian music halls to Josephine Baker's cabaret and the avant-garde ideas of Sadayakko Kawakami's crosscultural hybrids. Oskar Schlemmer at the Bauhaus and Vaslav Nijinsky in the Ballets Russes questioned conventional ideas about the costumed performing body. The subversive yet popular styling of David Bowie, Grace Jones and Prince continues to inspire musicians and designers alike.

From the Copper Age to the Digital Age, *The Fashion Chronicles* travels across five thousand years to chart the style stories of a hundred of the best-dressed people in history. By shining a spotlight on the place of fashion in our heritage, we place it in a wider cultural, political and social sphere, ultimately proving that true style never lacks substance.

Ancient

Eve

Created from Adam's rib, Eve, in the biblical telling of the fall of man, is the root cause of original sin. As recounted in Genesis 3.7 (King James Bible), after eating the forbidden fruit, 'the eyes of them both were opened, and they knew that they *were* naked; and they sewed fig leaves together, and made themselves aprons.' The story of Adam and Eve is crucial to many ideas around clothing, modesty and morality, but also appoints Eve as one of the first fashion designers, as sardonically noted by columnist Elsa Maxwell in American *Vogue* in 1934: 'Eve...became the first couturière, when she evidenced such striking concern as to the proper angle in the draping of her fig leaf.'[1]

The fig leaf became a symbol of censorship and moral propriety with enormous repercussions for the history of art. Statues in classical antiquity were often nude, modelled on naked athletes in a display of beauty and good citizenship. But with the rise of Christianity, moral ideals based on the Garden of Eden story had less tolerance for the naked human form. This was formalized in 1563 when the Roman Catholic Council of Trent ruled that 'all lasciviousness be avoided' in religious images.[2] This led to the 'fig leaf campaign', which saw painted or cast leaves deployed as a weapon in the war against indecency. As such, Eve's legacy can be found in museums, galleries, churches and cathedrals the world over. The first nude statue to be displayed in the UK since the Roman era was erected in 1822 in Hyde Park as part of the Wellington Monument. The 5.5-m (18-ft) statue of Achilles was created from melted-down French cannon and included a prudently placed fig leaf, the subject of much satire at the time.

The fruits of Eve's labour were celebrated in the early days of the silver screen. *Fig Leaves* (Howard Hawks, 1926) centres on the lives of a married couple: Adam and his fashion-obsessed wife Eve. Drawing on the idea of Eve as the original couturière, feted costume designer Adrian created fifty ensembles for a Technicolor fashion show sequence, which the *Los Angeles Times* described as 'the most original and vivid array of gowns ever shown on the screen.'[3] More recently, Vivienne Westwood has used the fig leaf as a recurring motif in her designs to signify environmental issues and moral hypocrisy.[4]

Humans have been adorning themselves for millennia. In 1991, tourists discovered a body as they were walking in the Ötztal Alps along the Austrian–Italian border. It turned out to be the oldest frozen mummy ever found. Further inspection showed that his final moments were traumatic: he was shot by an arrow in the back and suffered a severe blow to the head. Theories as to why he met such a sudden and violent death range from ritual sacrifice to the political machinations of a younger rival. Named Ötzi, he has been intriguing scientists, archaeologists and historians ever since.

leading them to surmise that he was part of an agricultural farming society rather than a more primitive hunter-gatherer group.[5] The mixture of skins, from presumably farmed animals to wild creatures, implies that his choices were not only based on ease of availability, but also on specific attributes provided by different animals to offer, for example, better protection from the elements or more flexibility. As unfounded in science as it may be, perhaps an element of aesthetic choice also played a part in selecting what to wear in the Tyrolean snow more than 5,000 years ago.

Ötzi the Iceman
c.3500–3100BCE

At least five different animals comprised the Iceman's clothing, including sheep and goat hides stitched together to make a coat, a bear fur hat and goat-leather leggings. What makes Ötzi especially well dressed is not his rudimentary couture skills, nor his mix-and-match approach, but the fact that analysing his clothing tells us so much about the life of this prehistoric man. Studies of the varieties of animal skin that made up his Copper Age wardrobe have provided scientists with clues to the type of society in which he lived,

Ötzi is adorned with 61 tattoos that are made up of groups of horizontal and vertical lines and Xs. They were likely made by rubbing charcoal into cuts and are thought to have been medicinal rather than decorative. Proving that fashion truly is cyclical, replicas of Ötzi's boots, made of deer, calf and bear leather, were created by a Czech academic, who told the *Telegraph*: 'Because the shoes are actually quite complex I'm convinced that even 5,300 years ago people had the equivalent of a cobbler who made shoes for other people.'[6] The shoes are now available commercially as OTZ Shoes, established in 2009.

In 1921, Thomas Thomsen excavated an oak-log coffin found in a burial mound in Egtved, near Vejle in Denmark. The coffin contained the remains of a girl aged between 16 and 18, who had been fully dressed for burial, placed on a cow hide and covered with a blanket. She was buried with an awl, a comb made of horn, a hairnet, a bucket that had once held a fermented drink (likely beer sweetened with honey) and the cremated remains of a child aged 5 to 6. It was later dated as a Bronze Age burial from c.1370BCE.

Egtved Girl
c.1370BCE

The burial clothes consisted of a short tunic-style bodice in fine wool, with a knee-length wool cord or string skirt and a belt featuring a bronze plate decorated with spirals, which is thought to represent the sun. The cord or string skirt was about 38cm (15 inches) long and wrapped around the waist twice, reaching down towards the knees. There are a number of theories about this style of skirt, which has been found in other Nordic burials as well as in areas of Southern and Eastern Europe and on Neolithic figurines, making it one of the first garments depicted on humans aside from animal furs. As the skirt provides no warmth, and very little modesty, it may relate to marriage, sexual intercourse and childbearing. Homer's *Iliad*, from around 800BCE, corroborates this with the story of Hera donning a 'girdle set with an hundred tassels' to deflect Zeus's attention from the Trojan battles. Aphrodite lends her just such a girdle, created for 'love and lust and flirtation'. The plan is successful and Zeus is seduced away from Troy.[7]

Tests on Egtved Girl and her clothing shed new light on Bronze Age life. Isotope analysis of her teeth, fingernails, hair and clothing showed that she likely originated in southwest Germany around the Black Forest, and travelled throughout her life. The wool of her clothing was not produced locally, hinting at textile production as part of the economy. Researchers note that southern Germany and Denmark were dominant centres of power at the time, and it has been suggested that Egtved Girl was involved in a marriage to form an alliance to strengthen trade routes involving key commodities, such as Baltic amber, which could be found on the Danish coast and traded for bronze.[8]

Tutankhamun was a boy-pharaoh of the 18th Dynasty, whose gold and blue funerary mask has become an icon of Ancient Egypt. His golden treasures are known the world over, but less renowned are the textiles and clothing that make up the largest group of items from his tomb. In 1923, shortly after the discovery, Howard Carter wrote: 'The material from this tomb will be of supreme importance to the history of textile art and it needs very careful study.'[9]

Tutankhamun
c.1341–c.23 BCE

The collection included 145 loincloths, 12 tunics, 28 gloves, 25 head coverings and nearly 100 sandals, some of which were worked in gold. The hoard also featured elaborately beaded pieces, garments embellished with gold discs resembling sequins and even a fake leopard skin made of woven linen with appliqued spots. Loincloths formed the basis of the Ancient Egyptian wardrobe, but while an ordinary member of the population could expect 37 to 50 threads per inch, royal loincloths were much more luxurious at 200.[10] Our knowledge of Tutankhamun's textiles comes predominantly from the work of Dr Gillian Vogelsang-Eastwood at the Textile Research Centre in the Netherlands. She has been studying the collection since the early 1990s and has re-created garments to gain an understanding of ancient techniques.

Personal appearance was of enormous importance to the pharaohs, and titles such as Royal Wigmaker and Hairdresser, and Keeper of the Royal Wardrobe stretch back for millennia before Tutankhamun's time.[11] Cosmetics were indispensable for both men and women. The most famous Egyptian make-up – kohl to emphasize the eyes – was immortalized in a love poem around

1300BCE: 'My longing for you is my eye-paint, when I see you my eyes shine'. As well as making an aesthetic impact, it also had medicinal benefits: it helped to reduce glare from the sun and antiseptic properties provided relief from irritation.[12]

On discovering Tutankhamun's tomb in 1922, Howard Carter triggered a fresh wave of Egyptomania across art, design and fashion that filtered into many areas of popular culture.[13] American *Vogue* acknowledged this impact in September 1923, noting:

'Some months ago, the Pharaoh Tut–ankh–Amen stepped from the quiet darkness of the tomb into the noisy glare of modern publicity. From the divine mortal of three thousand six hundred years ago, he has become the familiar "King Tut" to the man in the street. Modern woman has adopted the designs and decorations invented by the ancient costumers of the Nile, adding to the fascination of her person the art and craft of the jewelers of old Thebes.'[14]

ΣΑΠΦΟ

Little is known of the Ancient Greek lyric poet Sappho, and only fragments of her poetry survive. Hailing from the island of Lesbos in the Aegean Sea, she was revered throughout the ancient world, with Plato declaring her 'the Tenth Muse'. Her sensual poetry has cast her as an enduring symbol of desire and love between women.

During Sappho's lifetime, women undertook weaving at home and fine, domestically produced textiles were a status symbol. However, a shift was underway, and luxuries such as Milesian cloaks and Lydian headbands and sandals were imported from abroad, impacting women's position in Greek society.[15] Sappho refers to clothing throughout her work. An indication that class and status were aligned with dress is evident in fragment 57, in which the rustic nature of country attire is linked to a lack of sophistication: 'What country woman bewitches your mind… dressed in a country stola…not knowing how to draw the rags over her ankles?'[16]

Other fragments note the sensual and erotic qualities of sheer cloth with references to 'see-through' fabric (*beudos*, fragment 155) and the flowing texture of a dancer's dress: 'sing of

Gongyla, while desire once again flies around you, the lovely one – for her dress excited you when you saw it; and I rejoice' (fragment 22).[17] This titillating dress is sometimes translated as 'drapery' or 'fold', so could relate to the *peplos* or *chiton*.

The *peplos* and *chiton*, along with the *himation* (cloak), were key components of the Ancient Greek wardrobe. They were each made from a single rectangle of fabric that was folded down one side then secured at the shoulders with stitches or pins known as *fibulae*. The *peplos* was folded over at the top to form an extra layer of draped fabric reaching below the waist. Usually made of heavier cloth, it is evident on Greek art from the Archaic and Classical periods. The *peplos* may have featured on Greek statuary even after it was no longer worn because it functioned as a marker of Greek identity and embodied traditional values.[18]

Drapery from Ancient Greece remains a perpetual source of inspiration for fashion designers. It can be found in the pleating of Mariano Fortuny in the early 20th century and in the drapery of Madame Grès in the 1940s.[19] In more recent years, designers from Karl Lagerfeld to Jean Paul Gaultier have turned to influences from Classical and Archaic Greece, while Sophia Kokosalaki has drawn on her own Greek heritage to reimagine ancient drapery for the 21st century.

Sappho
c.620–570BCE

In 1971, a Han dynasty tomb was discovered that contained the exceptionally well-preserved body of Xin Zhui, also known as Lady Dai, the wife of a high-ranking official in Hunan Province, China. She had been buried with more than one thousand items to ensure her luxurious lifestyle continued in the afterlife. Many of these things were made from silk, highlighting the importance of the fabric in Chinese culture. Lady Dai was cocooned in twenty layers of silk and linen clothing, secured with silk bands, in a silk-lined coffin and covered with padded silk quilts. Silk brocade and embroidered silk adorned the outside of the coffin. Silk curtains, pillows, gowns, robes, gloves and shoes were found, as well as 46 rolls of the fabric.[20] Painted wooden figurines in the tomb depict silk fashions of the day. Thought to have been part of her funerary procession, an exquisitely painted silk sheet over 2m (6½ feet) long was draped over the coffin, decorated with fantastical creatures, gods and grotesques.[21]

Xin Zhui
c.213–163BCE

Silk cultivation dates back to the third millennium BCE in China, and the origins of sericulture are enshrined in mythology. The trade gave its name to the Silk Road, a system of commercial routes that joined the Far East to the Mediterranean, and China had a monopoly on silk production for at least a millennium and a half. During the Han dynasty, silk was so significant that it functioned as a form of unofficial currency; some civil servants even received their salaries in silk.[22]

Images of the tomb's discovery in 1971 tell a story about a very different point in history, also codified in dress. Workers clad in utilitarian blue 'Mao suits' and caps contrast with the lavish opulence inside the tomb. Predating Mao Zedong, the Sun Yat-sen uniform, as it is known in China, originated in the early years of the Chinese Republic, taking its name from the first president in 1912. Based on student uniforms, the suit forged a proletarian look that, while not regulated, created a collective identity in the People's Republic of China as Mao took power. The Cultural Revolution (1966–76) was an attack on anything considered 'un-Chinese'. Clothing became part of the battle, and Western suits were targeted along with modern Chinese styles such as the cheongsam. In the increasingly oppressive atmosphere, the Red Guards were known to attack people in the street for wearing inappropriate clothing, at times cutting off the offending articles with scissors.[23]

Reine Cléopâtre   208

Cleopatra VII was Queen of the Ptolemaic Kingdom of Egypt, a Macedonian-Greek dynasty descended from Alexander the Great's general Ptolemy, and the final Egyptian dynasty before the Roman conquest. Cleopatra was highly educated and spoke many languages. She bore children with Roman generals Julius Caesar and later Marc Antony, and her relationships with these men are often portrayed as some of history's most enigmatic love stories. Classical chroniclers believed she committed suicide by clasping an asp to her breast, an act that has been retold countless times. Some modern researchers, however, think it was more likely that she used poison.[24]

Cleopatra
69–30BCE

Throughout history Cleopatra has been depicted as the ultimate seductress, using her sorcerous charms to beguile men and vanquish her enemies. Unsurprisingly, Roman chroniclers perpetuated this representation during and after her lifetime, keen to paint her as a nefarious enchantress in the story of what would soon become the Roman Empire. The epic poem *Pharsalia* by Lucan, written around a century after Cleopatra's death, encapsulates the Roman view of Cleopatra. He called her,

'That disgrace of all Egypt,
Deadly scourge of the Latin race,
poison-seductress,
Of Rome.'

Lucan compares her 'ruinous beauty' to Helen of Troy. Her
clothing and jewellery – seen through a haze of poetic licence
and Roman propaganda – helped to cement the image of her
as a wanton temptress.

'Decked out in exceedingly deadly beauty…
Cleopatra wore a fortune plundered from the
Red Sea [pearls]
And her head and neck strained to support
Her adornments. Her breasts shined in Sidonian thread'[25]

Plutarch, writing at a similar time, claimed Cleopatra had
arrayed herself as Aphrodite, Greek goddess of love, when
she first met Marc Antony.[26]

Cleopatra soon became more archetype than person, a
blueprint for our ideas surrounding powerful women and the
way they present themselves in any age. Costuming Cleopatra
allowed for an opulent Orientalism in the case of the Ballets
Russes' *Cléopâtre* (1909), and she has long been a popular
figure for fancy dress and masquerade,[27] as seen in Marquise
de Chabannes's Cleopatra costume featured in American
Vogue in 1927 (*see* opposite). Other representations have
reflected the fashions of the day,[28] turning the Ptolemaic queen
into a contemporary parable, the supreme vamp. Cinematic
Cleopatras have enticed on the silver screen since the earliest
days of film, showing viewers the pinnacle of Hollywood excess,
from Cecil B DeMille's sumptuous spectacle (1934) to the lavish
extravagance of Elizabeth Taylor in 1963, each of which sparked
fashions for 'Egyptian' styles based on the fateful queen.[29]

Born Gaius Octavius Thurinus, Augustus was the adopted son and heir of Julius Caesar, and became the first Emperor of the Roman Empire in 27BCE. When he came to power, the toga was the ultimate sartorial emblem of Roman citizenship. According to Pliny the Elder, the lineage of the toga went back to the Etruscan kings, and both women and men wore it. Woven from wool, the toga supported the early domestic economy based on sheep herding.[30] While it was possible to import silk from China, it was viewed as a decadent luxury, so garments made entirely of silk were not considered appropriate for a legitimate emperor.[31]

To save the toga from decline, Augustus legislated that senators must wear it to the Forum to conduct public business, emphasizing its place in the social hierarchy. According to Roman historian Suetonius, Augustus invoked the poet Virgil, who had declared: 'The Romans, lords of the world, the nation clad in the toga!'[32] It became largely ceremonial dress, and increased in size to up to 5m (16½ft) wide. The swathes of drapery played an important role in the iconography of imperial statues.

Roman chroniclers linked strong statesmanship with sartorial propriety, often making reference to the toga. Controlling the drapery of the toga was seen as a metaphor for authority over the state and public affairs. Suetonius made this clear when he wrote of the emperor Caligula leaving a theatre in anger and tripping over his toga. This was one of many vestimentary examples that proved his inadequacy as a ruler.[33]

The Senate granted Augustus the right to wear a triumphal crown at important occasions, and he is often depicted with a laurel wreath around his head.[34] Mars, the god of war, also came to be associated with Augustus and his rule. This heroic image was created by depicting Augustus in the *cuirass* (a piece of armour formed of a breastplate and backplate).[35]

The dress of the Roman Republic and Empire was revived and revered in the aftermath of the French Revolution, in the last decade of the 18th century. The egalitarian ideals mixed with the aesthetics of recently excavated ancient statues to create a Neoclassical ideal that could be worn on the body in the form of white muslin gowns, or in cropped hair imitating the style of Roman busts in a celebration of democratic antiquity.[36]

Roman Emperor Augustus

63BCE—14CE

Boudicca, Queen of the Iceni people, led an uprising against the occupying Roman Empire in 60 or 61CE and, although defeated, became a folk hero in Britain. No evidence of writing from pre-Roman Britain has been found, so our understanding of clothing and culture from this period is drawn from archaeological evidence, alongside Roman sources who viewed the tribes of late Iron Age Britain as barbarians. No writing on Boudicca exists from her lifetime, but Cassius Dio, a Roman historian born nearly a century later, described the warrior queen as very tall and, 'in appearance most terrifying…a great mass of the tawniest hair fell to her hips; around her neck was a large golden necklace; and she wore a tunic of diverse colours over which a thick mantle was fastened with a brooch.'[37] While some historians suggest that Dio was exaggerating for dramatic effect,[38] some of these adornments certainly existed in 1st-century Britain.

Boudicca

c.30–61CE

Brooches and necklaces such as torcs have been found at archaeological sites that predate the Roman occupation. The tunic of 'diverse colours' could have been a stripe, check or tartan, and an excavation in Colchester did find a fragment of checked purple and white cloth.[39] Clothing could have come in a number of colours, from cream or brown unbleached wool to vegetable or animal dyes in red, yellow, blue and purple.[40] Natural dyes, especially blue derived from the woad plant, are central to the popular image of Boudicca as a warrior queen painted in battle to scare the enemy. This impression was formed in part by Julius Caesar the century before Boudicca's rebellion, when he claimed that blue woad was used to enhance the Britons' 'terrifying appearance in battle'.[41] This has sparked much debate. With limited archaeological evidence, the records come from Roman accounts, which were keen to emphasize how uncivilized Britons were. Sources such as Ovid, Pliny and Tacitus all noted that Britons stained their bodies, a practice seen as barbarous to Roman sensibilities. If skin *was* coloured, it could have been for decoration, for medical reasons such as disinfectant or, indeed, for going into battle.[42]

Today woad is grown and harvested in Norfolk by a company creating a range of products dyed with the natural pigment.[43] British fashion label Boudicca, named after the warrior queen of ancient Britain, was one of its first clients.[44]

C.H.S. del.ᵗ

Aquatinted by R. Havell

Boadicea, Queen   *of the Iceni.*

Medieval
5–15th Century

Theodora became Empress of the Byzantine Empire through her marriage to Emperor Justinian I. The key chronicler of her time, the scholar Procopius of Caesarea, wrote two very conflicting accounts of her rise to power. The official version portrays Theodora as pious and politically influential. The unpublished account, likely written with political disillusionment and deploying rhetorical spin, would make a 21st-century tabloid blush with its salacious stories and detailed debauchery. Procopius tells us that Theodora came from humble beginnings as a courtesan and actress, which is backed up by another contemporary, John of Ephesus, who describes her as 'from the brothel', at a time when a profession on the stage and sex work were viewed as interchangeable. Theodora's meteoric rise required Justinian, himself from a peasant family, to introduce special legislation to enable them to marry, and she welcomed her friends from the theatre into the palace throughout her reign.[1]

A lasting image of this compelling empress is found in the mosaics of Theodora and Justinian in the 6th-century Basilica of San Vitale in Ravenna, Italy. Both emperor and empress are depicted in high-ranking *chlamys* (cloaks) in imperial purple, a colour associated with wealth and power since antiquity. Theodora's cloak has an embroidered gold border at the bottom featuring the Adoration of the Magi. She reportedly referenced her robes in defense of her husband at the time of the Nika riots in 532, claiming: 'May I never be without the purple I wear, nor live to see the day when men do not call me "Your Majesty".'[2] Over the *chlamys*, Theodora wears a jewelled collar, and on her head a crown made all the more dramatic by pendilia of pearls and gems that hang below her shoulders.[3] The *chlamys* was probably made from silk, as the silkworm was introduced from China to Europe during Justinian's reign, and he quickly set up a monopoly on its production in the West.[4]

The enigmatic Theodora has directly inspired fashion collections from Romeo Gigli (Autumn/Winter 1989–90) and Karl Lagerfeld at Chanel (Paris-Byzance, Pre-Fall 2011). The Ravenna mosaic is also brought to mind in Dolce & Gabbana's Autumn/Winter 2013-14 collection that drew on the later mosaics at the Sicilian Cathedral of Monreale.

Theodora Empress of the Byzantine Empire
c.500–548CE

Called by some the 'Father of Europe' and hailing from the Carolingian dynasty, Charlemagne was King of the Franks. In 800 he was crowned Emperor of the Romans by Pope Leo III, forming the basis of what became the Holy Roman Empire. This was a momentous occasion as he became the first emperor in Western Europe since the fall of Rome, marking the start of two empires in Europe: Byzantine in the East, centred on Constantinople, and Carolingian in the West. Charlemagne had a love of learning, establishing schools in monasteries and cathedrals. But he was also a medieval warrior, expanding his lands through massacre and warfare and violently forcing conversion to Christianity.

Charlemagne
c.742–814

A courtier and scholar named Einhard, Charlemagne's contemporary biographer, described him as tall and well built, with fair hair and piercing eyes.[5] Einhard also recorded his dress in unusual detail for the time, telling us that Charlemagne wore the national dress common to all Franks: a linen shirt and breeches next to his skin, covered by a silk-fringed tunic, a cloak and a short jacket of otter or marten skins in the winter. The only time he diverged

significantly from the dress of his subjects was on feast days when he might have carried a jewelled sword and 'made use of embroidered clothes and shoes bedecked by a golden buckle, and he appeared crowned with a diadem of gold and gems, but on other days his dress varied little from the common dress of the people.'[6]

Einhard also noted that Charlemagne 'despised foreign costumes, however handsome', only allowing himself to be clothed in unfamiliar styles when in Rome, at the behest of the Pope, where he adopted the Roman tunic and *chlamys* (cloak).[7] However, one of his most versatile garments, the cloak, was imported from England. Correspondence between Charlemagne and Offa, King of Mercia (an Anglo-Saxon kingdom in England) reveals that the Frankish king complained that the cloaks were getting smaller: 'Our people make a demand about the size of the cloaks, that you may order them to be such as used to come to us in former times.'[8] The cloak functioned as a blanket as well as protection from the elements. It became a point of contention for Charlemagne when shorter styles gained favour, as captured in a later account: 'When I go off to empty my bowels, I catch cold because my backside is frozen.'[9]

ODO:EPS: ROTBE[

WIL[ELM:

Also known as King William I and William the Bastard, in British history William of Normandy earned his name as the Conqueror for his triumph over Harold II at the Battle of Hastings in 1066. The battle was the culmination of a succession crisis after the death of Edward the Confessor. The Normans made an extensive cultural impact on Anglo-Saxon society, affecting the nobility, clergy, architecture and language.

William the Conqueror
c.1028–87

The best-known representation of William is on the Bayeux Tapestry (technically an embroidery), the most celebrated example of Anglo-Saxon art, assuming, as most scholars do, that it is the product of Anglo-Saxon craftsmanship. The wool-on-linen embroidery is nearly 70m (230ft) long, and many contemporary scholars believe its patron was Bishop Odo of Bayeux, William's half-brother.[10] There is political ambiguity throughout the piece, which makes attribution somewhat difficult. Although it is sympathetic to Harold in places, it is likely meant as a form of Norman propaganda. Is it to be considered art, craft, a political tract or a historical record? Created for display in a cathedral or castle, the embroidery was arguably a fashionable item in its own right.

The needlework distinguishes between English and Norman figures by differences in clothing and grooming. The English have moustaches while the Normans are clean-shaven with shaved hair at the back of the head. This may reflect contemporary styles, or could be an artistic conceit to identify the two opposing sides. The English generally wear tunics while the Normans wear culottes, perhaps to highlight the equestrian prowess of the Norman warriors as Anglo-Saxons were unaccustomed to horseriding.[11]

Long believed to have been the work of Queen Matilda, William's wife, the embroidery is now mostly considered to be the creation of English needleworkers, probably women, possibly nuns in Canterbury, as there was already a tradition of embroidery there that would flourish in following centuries (see Pope Boniface VIII, page 50). Competence at needlework was a marker of fashionably refined middle- and upper-class femininity in the 19th century,[12] an association that saw embroidery denigrated as 'women's work', as a lowly craft rather than respected 'fine art'. So ingrained did this opinion become that when the Royal Academy was established it would not admit needlework.[13] The depiction of William the Conqueror on the Bayeux Tapestry illuminates not only medieval clothing, but also the history of women and textile arts.

The most powerful woman in 12th-century Europe, Eleanor of Aquitaine married two kings, and was queen of both France and England. At a young age she inherited roughly a third of modern France, from the Loire to the Pyrenees, becoming an incredibly eligible marriage prospect. She married King Louis VII of France at the age of 15, and even joined him on the Second Crusade. A few weeks after their marriage was annulled, Eleanor married Henry Plantagenet who became King Henry II of England. They had eight children, two of whom became reining kings of England. Eleanor spent later years under house arrest after siding with her sons in a failed revolt against the king, but after Henry's death she acted as regent when her sons were fighting abroad. She was also instrumental in negotiating marriages to secure the dynasty across Europe.

Eleanor of Aquitaine
c.1122–1204

While it is difficult to piece together a picture of Eleanor's early life due to lack of evidence, later accounts and chronicles suggest she enjoyed fine clothes, was a lover of jewellery and often wore silk embroidered with gold thread.[14] The court of Eleanor's childhood, in the medieval region of Aquitaine in southwest France, was a sophisticated centre of culture and fashion. It was here that troubadour traditions of lyric poetry expressing courtly love developed, which have often been linked to Eleanor. Areas further north, at times, considered the region and its inhabitants profligate in their love of finery and poetry.

The abbot Bernard of Clairvaux took a dim view of Eleanor's luxurious fashions, disapproving of her 'queenly splendour'. He complained that women of the court 'drag after them trains of precious material that make a cloud of dust. Some you see are not so much adorned as loaded down with ornaments of gold, silver and precious stones.'[15] Court dress during Eleanor's lifetime consisted of an ensemble known as the *bliaut girone*. Worn with a decorative girdle or belt, it was cut in two pieces, drawn tight with ribbons through the torso and with wide, falling skirts. Eleanor wears the *bliaut girone* in her wax seal.[16] The sleeves were the most distinctive feature: tight from shoulder to elbow and flaring out to enormous lengths that could trail on the ground.[17] This silhouette forms an image of the medieval woman that endures in the popular imagination, helped by the enthusiasm of Pre-Raphaelite artists in the 19th century.

ELEONOR OF ACQUITAINE.

Queen consort of   Henry 2nd of England.

Married 1150.   Died 1204.

An authentic portrait engraved   *exclusively for the Court Magazine*

N.º 97 of the series   *of ancient portraits*

VOL. XX

In 1206 the warrior Temüjin was granted the title of 'Chinggis Khan' (Universal Ruler) at a meeting of Mongol leaders. He was on the verge of conquering and unifying an enormous empire, which expanded under his sons to reach from Eastern Europe to the East China Sea and from Siberia to the Persian Gulf, in what has been called the world's first land superpower.[18]

Genghis Khan
c.1162–1227

The Silk Road is a relatively modern term for the historical interconnecting routes of trade and cultural exchange. Named after a product that frequently traversed its paths, the Silk Road has also acted as a transport route for crops, religions, languages and even diseases. These networks across Central Eurasia were strengthened and organized under Genghis Khan and the empire that grew in his wake, to include systems of taxation and sophisticated communications in an economic structure that linked China to Southeast Asia, India, Africa and the Mediterranean.

Some historians have suggested that one of the primary aims of the early raids that preceded the empire was to seize precious cloths (along with gold and women).[19] Interest in the trade and manufacture of

wearable wealth, such as *nasij* (cloth of gold), flourished as the empire expanded. This contrasted with the pre-Genghis wardrobe of nomadic Mongols, which included textiles such as felt, wool, camel hair and leather.[20] A Persian historian of the 13th century claimed that Mongols were adorned in 'the skins of dogs and mice' before Genghis Khan. This was exaggerated, but the preferred skins were readily available fox, lynx and wolf.[21] Skilled textile workers were transferred to Central Asia from all over the empire to create fine fabrics for the ruling powers to wear and trade. The desire for luxury textiles was also a yearning for status and legitimacy.

Genghis Khan's horseback armies wrought immense destruction. The impact was even felt on the global climate: cultivation in China was abandoned at such extensive rates that carbon-dioxide emissions were affected.[22] The artistic legacy was far-reaching, and included new idioms of design and textile manufacture.[23] The high heel is one of many cultural legacies of the Mongol empire, and was worn by Persian and Mongolian riders as an equestrian aid to secure the foot in the stirrup. Stacked leather heeled boots probably came to Europe through the Mongol invasions or the Crusades. Associated with wealth and power, they soon entered court circles and were worn by the likes of Louis XIV four centuries later.[24]

Pope Boniface VIII (born Benedetto Caetani) was pope from 1294 until his death in 1303. A controversial figure in his lifetime (some claimed his predecessor had resigned under pressure from Boniface), he was often in conflict with foreign rulers, especially the King of France, over the issue of papal versus monarchical power. Accusations of corruption surrounded him and led Italian poet Dante to suggest in his narrative poem, *The Divine Comedy*, that Boniface would end up in the Eighth Circle of Hell for abusing his ecclesiastical privileges for profit.

Pope Boniface VIII
c.1230–1303

Boniface was a great patron of *Opus Anglicanum*, or 'English work', which refers to the very high-quality English embroidery of the period. Embroidery signified the height of luxury in medieval Europe, and English embroidery enjoyed an international reputation. It was prized at royal courts and was commissioned by ecclesiastics for use on liturgical vestments. Boniface was both a giver and receiver of *Opus Anglicanum*. Elaborate embroidery was often bequeathed to churches, and, on becoming pope, Boniface presented garments to the cathedral of his native city Anagni. In 1295 King Edward I gave him an embroidered cope (a cloak-like liturgical vestment). He was also buried in his finery. When his tomb was opened in the early 17th century, his body was covered in a gold-embroidered vestment portraying scenes of the Infancy and Passion of Christ.[25]

In 1295 King Edward I gave
him an embroidered cope.

Such diplomatic gifts and a taste for ostentation were not always viewed favourably. The fashion for including a personal coat of arms in embroidery designs, so that the donor could be acknowledged, was criticized, and monastic orders attempted (largely unsuccessfully) to reduce the display of heraldry in churches. A papal inventory of 1311 noted a number of embroideries that included the family arms of none other than Boniface VIII.[26]

In secular life, the sumptuous nature of embroidery is illustrated by the English royal embroiderers, who did not stitch alongside the royal tailors but instead worked for the armourers at the Tower of London, probably because of the use of gold and silver thread.[27] The links between embroidery and refinement are clear in the general prologue to Geoffrey Chaucer's *Canterbury Tales*, written almost a century later between 1387 and 1400. The Squire, son of the Knight, is a paragon of chivalric elegance, covered in floral emblems:

'Embrouded was he, as it were a meede
Al ful of fresshe floures, whyte and reede.'
(Embroidered as if he were a meadow
All full of fresh flowers, white and red.)

The son of Edward III, Edward the Black Prince was a knight of the Plantagenet dynasty. As a warrior prince, Edward led the English to victory in some of the earliest battles of the Hundred Years' War, after his father staked his claim to the French throne by publically assuming the title 'King of England and France' in 1340, a move that sparked a long and bloody conflict.

Edward,
The Black Prince
1330–76

Clothing in the 14th century was undergoing seismic changes, much of it led by the monarchy. Chroniclers noted that by the middle of the century, fashions were beginning to change on a yearly basis and had become much tighter and shorter, with jagged edges and long hoods that used excessive and ostentatious amounts of fabric. These new-fangled fashions were the subject of much moralizing, and contemporary chroniclers of the time regularly blamed this apparent decadence for natural disasters and lost battles. 'To tell the truth,' wrote John of Reading, 'they looked more like tormentors and devils in their clothes and appearance than men. And the women copied the men in even more curious ways: for their clothes were so tight that they sewed foxtails beneath their clothes to hang down and protect and hide their arses.'[28]

The Black Prince's contribution to fashion history is the clothing left in his will. Written the day before he died, he left specific instructions for his funeral and tomb, ordering certain items to be carried during the procession and left on display. Accordingly, a number of pieces, including a military 'jupon' (a padded overcoat), were hung over his tomb in Canterbury Cathedral for nearly six hundred years,[29] and still remain in the collections of the cathedral today. The jupon, a type of 'linen armour' worn as a protective outer layer that helped to shield the metal beneath from attacking arrows, was a symbol of Edward's status as military hero.

Crucially, the jupon was quartered with heraldic emblems of the French and English, the fleur-de-lys and the leopard, respectively, to show Edward's family's claim to the French crown. Heraldry was of utmost importance to medieval rulers to communicate status and power through visual identity. It was vital to ensure troops could see their leaders on the battlefield. It also conveyed chivalric principles through luxuriant fabrics and detailing. Made from red and blue velvet with gold embroidery, the Black Prince's jupon was certainly a glaring statement, and one of the few pieces of 14th-century clothing in existence today.

Chroniclers of the time regularly blamed this apparent decadence for natural disasters and lost battles.

Joan of Arc

1412–31

When just a teenager, Joan of Arc had a series of visions that compelled her to support the military campaign of Crown Prince Charles of Valois, heir to the French throne, in his fight against the English during the Hundred Years' War. She was captured and burned at the stake in 1431. Her trial for heresy focused in part on her adoption of male clothes, drawing on the Old Testament verse: 'The woman shall not wear that which pertaineth unto a man, neither shall a man put on a woman's garment: for all that do so are abomination unto the LORD thy God.'[30] As one of the major charges brought against her dealt with her dress, there are many records we can draw on to understand what she wore.

Her cropped hair and clothing were seen as immodest and unnatural, and included short tunics, tabards 'open at the sides' and a cloak of gold: 'having cast aside all womanly decency...she had worn the apparel and garments of most dissolute men, and, in addition, had some weapons of defence.'[31] She was called a monstrous woman for cross-dressing and bearing arms,[32] but the clothing she donned in battle, at court and in prison also flouted the rules of social hierarchy. Born a peasant, the 'Maid of Orleans' not only dressed as a soldier, but also as a knightly courtier. Chronicles of the time describe her 'very noble clothes of cloth-of-gold and silk well trimmed with fur', a lavish blue hat with gold embroidery, a dark green tunic and embroidered nettle leaves to represent the monarch. Charges at her trial noted these 'sumptuous and magnificent clothes of precious fabrics and gold'.[33]

Joan's use of men's clothing was not only for practical reasons. She also believed it was the will of God, allowing her to enter into combat while also signalling her chastity. She refused to relinquish men's dress, even on pain of death, claiming, 'when I have done what I was sent to do by God, I will take women's clothes'.[34] Joan of Arc was canonized in 1920, five hundred years after she was burned to death, and is today a patron saint of France. Alexander McQueen drew on her style legacy in his 'Joan' collection (Autumn/Winter 1998–9), which featured a model trapped in a ring of flames for its finale.

Early Modern

15th–mid 18th Century

Painting of Giovanni di Nicolao Arnolfini & Costanza Trenta

1434

The 'Arnolfini portrait', painted by Jan van Eyck in 1434, is possibly the most debated portrait in Western art history. Speculation over the subjects of the painting has raged for hundreds of years and there are extensive theories behind the purpose of the painting.[1] Latest arguments suggest that the couple in the picture are Italian cloth merchant Giovanni di Nicolao Arnolfini and his wife Costanza Trenta (who had died the year before), in their home in Bruges.

What is undeniable is that the luxurious clothing on display speaks of the subjects' vast wealth. Medieval Bruges was a centre of commerce, with strategic links to northern European and Mediterranean trade routes, an area that has been called the cradle of capitalism.[2] As merchants, the Arnolfinis were at the vanguard of shifts in society that saw an element of social mobility begin to develop. Riches could be achieved through trade and not just by accident of birth, which led to sumptuary laws in many European countries. These laws were used to denote status in a society where mobility was feared, clearly demarcating social standing as well as encouraging domestic industry.[3] Fur-lined fabrics exquisitely dyed in vivid green, blue and deep black indicate the affluence of the Arnolfinis. The gown cascades on the floor in an ostentatious display of abundance, the fabric a high-quality wool that may have cost more than silk.[4]

Scholars have debunked the myth that the woman in the painting is pregnant, despite her appearance. In 1841, the year before the portrait was bought by the National Gallery, a critic in the literary journal *The Athenaeum* perpetuated the idea of pregnancy by implying a shotgun wedding, noting the woman has 'one hand on her stomacher like a lady who had "loved her lord" six months ere he became so'.[5] What becomes clear when studying the painting alongside its contemporaries is that the distended stomach was not a marker of pregnancy, but rather an idealized version of the female body that was present in saintly virgins as well as secular portraits. Likened by some art historians to the swelling arches of late gothic architecture, it is unusual in its deviation from classical ideals of beauty.[6] It is arguably another marker of fashionability and an excuse to parade even more swathes of fabric.

Oba Ewuare, also known as Ewuare the Great, ruled the Kingdom of Benin (Edo) in modern-day Nigeria in the mid-15th century. The Oba (divine king) was the pinnacle of Benin society, with power over the life and death of his subjects. The first of the warrior kings in Benin, Ewuare is an important figure in oral histories. Described as 'a great magician, doctor, traveller, and warrior',[7] Ewuare expanded the empire, rebuilding the city and royal palace after they were destroyed in a conflict with his brother, and organizing guilds for services to the crown, from leopard hunters to textile workers. He instigated administrative and civic changes that improved stability throughout the kingdom. As part of this restructuring, he is said to have introduced annual ceremonies to honour ancestors and protect the domain.[8]

Royal regalia developed alongside these ceremonial rituals, the most important of which were coral beads. Legend has it that Ewuare stole beads that belonged to Olokun, god of the waters, to establish himself as his counterpart, king of the dry land. Ewuare also founded the office of *Iwebo*,

Oba Ewuare,
King of Benin
reigned 1440 – c.1473/80

set up to guard the Oba's regalia, beads and wardrobe.[9] Coral beads were subject to strict regulation. A complete outfit of beads netted together was restricted to the king alone, forming a vital part of the paraphernalia of royalty that remains in use by the current Oba today. The beads were infused with the magical power of *ase*: whatever is said in possession of them will come to pass.[10] Coral beads became so interwoven with kingship that a chief could not visit the king unless adorned with a coral necklace, and losing a coral bead was once punishable by death.[11]

Under Oba Ewuare's rule, society was transformed and the arts flourished. The guilds that performed services for the king constituted an artisan class that built on earlier groups such as *owina n'ido*, the royal weavers' guild, which created decorative patterned textiles.[12] Ewuare also expanded the art of brass casting in Benin, introducing commemorative heads to honour previous rulers.[13] Previously, brass casting had been used for such small items as jewellery, but workshops were established in the palace grounds and brass casters became highly respected artisans. Violent colonization by the British in 1897 led to the plundering of much brass and bronze artwork, and had a profoundly detrimental impact on the dress cultures of the region,[14] with many artifacts remaining in the British Museum today.

POTENTISSIMVS MAXIMVS ET INVICTISSIMVS CÆSAR MAXIMILIANVS
QVI CVNCTOS SVI TEMPORIS REGES ET PRINCIPES IVSTICIA PRVDENCIA
MAGNANIMITATE LIBERALITATE PRÆCIPVE VERO BELLICA LAVDE ET
ANIMI FORTIDVDINE SVPERAVIT NATVS EST ANNO SALVTIS HVMANÆ
M·CCCC·LIX·DIE·MARCII·IX·VIXIT ANNOS·LIX·MENSES·IX·DIES·XXV
DECESSIT VERO ANNO M·D·XIX·MENSIS IANVARII DIE·XII· QVEM DEVS
OPT·MAX·IN·NVMERVM·VIVENCIVM·REFERRE·VELIT·

One of the most powerful rulers in Europe, Holy Roman Emperor Maximilian I was known as 'the last of the knights',[15] and referred to himself as the White King. He promoted the chivalric code through his interest in jousting tournaments, hunting and the other pursuits of a courtly lifestyle. A great patron of the arts, Maximilian commissioned a series of woodcuts to glorify his life, and he co-authored an autobiographical novel to ensure that he would be enshrined in history as brave, cultivated and highly educated. This is captured in the accompanying verse to one of the woodcuts:

Maximilian I,
Holy Roman Emperor
1459–1519

'Much of his time was nobly spent
In the true knightly tournament,
A source of valor and elation;
Therefore, upon his instigation,
With knightly spirit and bold heart
I have improved this fighting art.'[16]

Maximilian's patronage of the arts intersected with his interest in jousting and warfare through his love of armour. In 1504 he established a royal armoury at Innsbruck, Austria, which became one of the finest centres of armour manufacture in the world. The Emperor even styled himself as an expert armourer in his autobiographical novel, *Der Weisskunig* (The White King), claiming, 'he learned so industriously that he understood all the masterpieces of armour manufacture and even discovered many new art-concepts that were hidden from others'.[17]

The influence of Maximilian's taste in armour certainly had a far-reaching effect. Even King Henry VIII of England admired Maximilian's armour. In 1511, just two years after ascending the throne, Henry commissioned his own armour from Maximilian's Master Armourer, Konrad Seusenhofer. That same year work began on a monumental tournament armour set, commissioned by Maximilian as a gift for Henry. The only piece that exists today is an extraordinary horned helmet.[18] There is some debate as to whether the horns and spectacles are original, but they date from at least 1547. Aggrieved that English armour manufacturers were neither as skilled nor as prolific as their Continental counterparts, in 1511 Henry began to assemble his own royal armoury near the palace of his birth in Greenwich. He recruited Flemish, Milanese and German armourers to produce armour with its own distinctive style.

Armour for parades, jousts and battles was an intrinsic part of the fashionable courtier's wardrobe. Plate armour often followed the fashion of clothing, as details such as fabric folds and ornamentation could be transposed on to metal. Later in the century, courtiers used the magnificent designs by the Greenwich armourers to vie for the attention of Henry's daughter, Queen Elizabeth I.

Moctezuma II
1466–1520

Moctezuma II ruled the Mesoamerican empire, broadly referred to as Aztec, in modern-day Mexico.[19] In 1519 the era of European colonization was accelerated with the arrival of Spanish conquistador Hernán Cortés in the Aztec capital of Tenochtitlán. Much has been written about the encounter between Cortés and Moctezuma, and the subsequent defeat of the indigenous ruler. On meeting, gifts were exchanged between the two. Moctezuma's gifts, including a beaded cape, two feather headdresses and shields, showcased the exquisite work of local artisans and were interpreted by Cortés as a sign that Moctezuma believed him to be a god, and therefore the rightful ruler. It has been suggested however, that they could have been the precursors to Cortés becoming a ritual sacrifice.[20]

Precolonial Aztec society was highly stratified. Dress and adornment were key signifiers of status, as illustrated by Moctezuma's gifts. Sumptuary laws and regulations were created to enforce these distinctions, including the decree that: 'Only the king is to wear the fine mantles of cotton embroidered with designs and threads of different colors and featherwork.'[21] Cotton was a high-status fabric, while commoners were expected to dress in maguey, yucca or palm fibres.[22] On occasion, Moctezuma wore the official cape of the Aztec rulers, emblazoned with a geometric design in blue. The cape most probably symbolized his genealogy and therefore legitimacy to rule, much like heraldry operated in some European countries.[23]

European contact with the 'New World' was documented in costume books to create an image of exoticized ethnicity from the 16th century onwards.[24] Indigenous cultures throughout the Americas used feathers for ceremonial and decorative reasons, and Central American Aztec featherwork, particularly when it incorporated iridescent quetzal feathers, could have symbolic and spiritual meaning. Professional feather artisans, known as *amantecas*, created royal and ceremonial clothing using intricate techniques.[25]

When treasure from Aztec Mexico was sent to Europe, it was packed with Tupinambá pieces (from present-day Brazil), and to European eyes they were all viewed with the same romantic wonder. As such, feathers became signifiers of anything non-European. At a point when European colonialism was escalating, Moctezuma, his dress (real or imagined) and his court became emblems of the exotic yet noble 'savage' that could be 'civilized' by European Christian values.

Principal adviser to King Henry VIII, Thomas Cromwell played a crucial role in the Reformation, a pivotal moment in English history. He was responsible for the dissolution of the monasteries after the split from Rome, and was a key figure in the execution of Henry VIII's second wife Anne Boleyn. Cromwell's father made a living from a number of trades, from fulling cloth to blacksmithing and keeping a tavern. In his youth, Thomas spent time in Europe, where he became a self-taught lawyer. On his return to England, he progressed prodigiously, becoming chief minister to King Henry VIII, a Knight of the Garter and, briefly, the Earl of Essex before his downfall and execution.

Thomas Cromwell
c.1485–1540

The court of Henry VIII was a stage upon which the theatre of monarchy was enacted, with clothing playing a vital role in creating an image of sovereign power. On his death in 1547, the King had an inventory that listed 40 gowns, 13 Spanish cloaks and 8 other cloaks, 26 doublets and 25 pairs of hose, in a range of colours that included orange,

russet, yellow, green, purple, crimson, gold and silver, a much brighter array than others in his household. Foreign ambassadors sent reports on the King's clothing back to their home courts. Henry did not take criticism lightly, as one observer noted at Anne Boleyn's trial, 'she was also charged, and her brother likewise, with having laughed at the king and his dress'.[26]

Against the backdrop of the magnificence of the Tudor court, Cromwell's rise and fall can be tracked through his dress. Inventories of Cromwell's clothing in the late 1520s, before he reached the pinnacle of his ascendancy, show a substantial wardrobe, but one mostly befitting his status. The colours were dark and fur trimmings consisted of fox, rabbit, lamb and squirrel, all of which were produced in England. One item that stands out from Cromwell's sartorial sobriety is a 'purple satin doublet'. Purple was restricted to noble use and since antiquity had been associated with royalty, so this item perhaps hints at Cromwell's social aspirations. Later, as a Knight of the Garter, Cromwell spent £44 on a sable fur, a vast sum when it is thought that an average labourer earned less than £7 per year. When Cromwell was arrested, it was through his clothing that his detractors made their case, stripping his body of his Garter regalia as he was taken to the Tower.[27]

Süleyman the Magnificent

1494/95–1566

The 1453 capture of Constantinople by Ottoman forces marked the end of the Byzantine Empire. Under Süleyman's sultanate (1520–66) the Ottoman empire greatly expanded and a golden age of Ottoman culture began.

The magnificence of the Ottoman court reflected a textile production at its peak.[28] Flowing kaftans emphasized the exquisiteness of the fabric, rather than construction and cut, and offered a markedly different silhouette to fitted European fashions so that kaftans became markers of Ottoman identity.[29] Headgear signified gender, ethnicity, religion and status, and was a feature of Turkish dress even before the Islamic period saw the adoption of the turban.[30]

Süleyman's wardrobe conveyed the glory of the Ottoman court: kaftans adorned with pearls or lined with leopard skin, and turbans garnished with rubies.[31] Kaftans played an important role in statecraft, from diplomatic gifts (*hil'at*), a tradition that dated back to the Prophet Muhammad,[32] to the ritual of 'kaftaning the ambassador', robing foreign dignitaries before they entered the sultan's throne room. From the 16th century, the clothing of deceased sultans and princes was stored in the palace treasury. The Topkapı Palace holds a thousand kaftans, forming Europe's oldest dynastic dress collection.[33]

Süleyman formalized many dress codes and sumptuary laws. Religious identity was foregrounded, and non-Muslims were differentiated from the Muslim population through their dress. The turban was restricted to Muslims, while non-Muslims were only permitted to wear sombre colours like dark blue and black. Colours such as green, which had religious significance, were limited to particular Muslim groups.[34] Süleyman's piety was enshrined in talismanic shirts that were decorated with Quranic verses and prayers.[35]

The domination of the Ottoman Empire during Süleyman's reign saw Turkish influence, 'Turquerie', sweep through Western Europe due to military encounters and the circulation of woodcuts and miniatures. The influence of Islamic Ottoman headgear can be traced in headdresses in the West,[36] and Turkish inspiration was evident in the wardrobe of King Henry VIII, from the arabesque designs on his doublets to cassocks that reflected the cut of kaftans and 'Turquey gownes' of crimson velvet embroidered with gold and silver.[37]

Bess of Hardwick (also known as Elizabeth Cavendish, later Elizabeth Talbot, and the Countess of Shrewsbury) was a remarkable woman of the Tudor age, who rose from the gentry to the upper levels of the nobility through a succession of four marriages. Her legacy is found in the English country houses that she had a hand in building: Chatsworth House and Hardwick Hall, both in Derbyshire. A keen needlewoman, Bess commissioned and bought much textile art, from tapestries to grace her walls to intricate embroidery and some of the earliest examples of bobbin lace in the country to adorn herself and her family.[38]

Bess of Hardwick
c.1527–1608

Bess's love of needlework is evident in the gifts she gave to Queen Elizabeth I. Nobility and courtiers were expected to give New Year presents to the royal family, a tradition established by King Henry VIII. These gifts might include clothes made from sumptuous fabrics, such as the 'French gown' with a high bodice of black taffeta striped with gold and silver that Bess offered to Queen Elizabeth I in 1584.[39] The Hardwick portrait of Elizabeth I (c.1599, by Nicholas Hilliard, see overleaf) is thought to have been commissioned by Bess, and was possibly on display at Hardwick Hall during the Queen's lifetime. Depicting a gown embroidered with real and fantastical flora and fauna, the painting may be based on a dress given to the Queen by Bess, and she may even have designed the embroidery.

Floral motifs were important in Tudor times, from iconography in natural history books to conveying medicinal healing properties and political affiliations (for instance, the rose was associated with Tudor rule). Fragrance was also important. Elizabeth I's linens were scented with dried rose petals, and distilled flower oils scented her clothes and body. The poet, lawyer and politician Sir John Davies described Elizabeth in a poem as the 'Empresse of flowers'.[40]

Bess's legacy survives not only in the bricks and mortar of Chatsworth House and Hardwick Hall, but also in the textile collections that she bequeathed to her heirs in perpetuity, which now form the largest collection of 16th- and 17th-century textiles from a single private English family. They include pieces she worked on with Mary, Queen of Scots, who lived in the Shrewsbury residences during her period of house arrest. Inspired by the Tudor dynasty, Vivienne Westwood re-created the Hardwick portrait gown for her 'Five Centuries Ago' collection of Autumn/Winter 1997–8.

Floral motifs were important in Tudor times, from iconography in natural history books to conveying medicinal healing properties.

Throughout European history until the late 17th century, the country with the most political power often wielded the most influence in the fashion stakes. In 1556, Philip II became the King of Spain and its territories. Spanish influence was vast, and, due to its imperial expansion, it became the first empire to be described as one on which 'the sun never sets'.

King Philip II of Spain
1527—98

A particular style of Spanish dress was established under Philip II, which was spread and modified around other countries where he had authority. These styles were recognizable for their austerity, modesty and geometric cut, and Spanish tailors became renowned throughout Europe for their dexterity with cloth.[41] Philip was also briefly King of England when he married Queen Mary I, an uncomfortable pairing in part because she had initially been contracted to marry his father. Mary enjoyed fashion according to one contemporary who noted: 'She seems to delight above all in arraying herself elegantly and magnificently'.[42] When Philip arrived at the English court, he is credited

with sparking a trend for the 'Spanish cloak' with a decorative hood.[43]

Crucially for Philip's sartorial domination, black was the new black. His predilection for the colour has been read as evidence of his piety and stoicism, encapsulated in paintings of him by El Greco. It is sometimes attributed to the time he spent in mourning for his wives and children. There is also an argument that black was already embedded in Spanish culture, having become a marker of Catholic faith after the fall of Grenada when the practising of Islam and Judaism was outlawed.[44] Black as a national style was a form of propaganda.

Black was a common colour throughout Spain, associated with merchants and with the population as a whole; in some accounts the Spanish were described as *gente de capa negra* (black-coat people).[45] However, despite its associations with piety, modesty and trade, black also signified riches. It was incredibly expensive to dye successfully as colourfast techniques were rudimentary, and on most fabrics black faded quickly. Black was a colour of luxury and was only worn by people who could afford it. Furthermore, it acted as the perfect backdrop for precious gems and jewellery plundered from the 'New World'.

A favourite of Queen Elizabeth I of England, Robert Dudley was the man who came closest to marrying the Virgin Queen. There has been much speculation about the nature of the relationship between Elizabeth and Dudley, but most current historians think it is very unlikely that it was sexual. Scandal hit their relationship when Dudley's wife died in mysterious circumstances. Rumours of murder spread but no evidence was found, and the manner of her death is still debated today. Elizabeth made Dudley Master of the Horse, a Knight of the Garter and Earl of Leicester.

Robert Dudley, 1st Earl of Leicester
1532/3–88

There is no doubt that Dudley was an arbiter of taste and a supreme man of fashion at the Elizabethan court. He ran up debts with tailors and mercers, and in 1588 seven doublets and two cloaks of his were valued at £543, making each item more than William Shakespeare paid for a house.[46] Due to the prodigious spending on apparel and the extreme silhouettes that 16th-century fashion demanded, from padded 'peascod' or goose-bellied doublets to exaggerated ruffs, Elizabeth passed a number of proclamations to restrict what could be worn. Fashions changed rapidly, signifying a social order in flux.

Portraits of Leicester show him in variations of the Tudor fashion of ruff, doublet and trunk hose (short, full breeches). Reaching to mid-thigh, trunk hose were often paned (slashed into ribbon-like strips or constructed from ribbons of fabric) so that a contrasting lining could be seen beneath. To achieve the desired effect, trunk hose were padded and stuffed with horsehair or wool, leading to a proclamation banning 'monstrous and outrageous greatness of hose'.[47] Punishment for disobeying these sartorial regulations was confiscation, a fine and even time in jail. However, in reality, these laws were difficult to enforce, and it was more often tailors and hosiers that paid the price, rather than nobles or merchants.

The volume of the trunk hose contrasted with the slenderness of courtiers' legs. From the mid-16th century, knitted silk stockings were imported from Spain to encase a gentleman's exposed and shapely limbs, which were keen markers of virility and symbolic of courtly pursuits, such as dancing and riding. As noted by Shakespeare in *Much Ado About Nothing* (c.1598): 'With a good leg and a good foot... and money enough in his purse, such a man would win any woman in the world.'[40]

'A well-tied tie is the first serious step in life,' wrote Oscar Wilde in *A Woman of No Importance*, which premiered in 1893. Two-and-a-half centuries earlier, Croatian Baroque poet and playwright Ivan Gundulić was painted wearing the forerunner of the tie: the cravat. The style and etymology of the cravat is thought to date from the Thirty Years' War (1618–48), when it was worn by Croatian horseriding mercenaries fighting for the Imperial Army of the Holy Roman Empire. Legend has it that French soldiers were impressed by this sartorial flourish, and a style was born. 'Croat' is therefore popularly considered to be the origin of

Ivan Gundulić
1589—1638

the word 'cravat'.[49] seen in an alternative spelling in Daniel Defoe's *Memoirs of a Cavalier* (1720), which was set during the Thirty Years' War: 'we fell foul with 200 Crabats'.[50] To commemorate this lineage, Cravat Day is celebrated annually on 18 October in Croatia; it debuted in 2003 to advertise the country and lock in its reputation as 'inventor' of the necktie.

In the second half of the 17th century, kings, cousins and trendsetters Louis XIV of France and Charles II of England became fans of the cravat or jabot worn at the neck. Meanwhile,

warfare continued to be an influence on the style. The Battle of Steenkerque in 1692, part of the Nine Years' War, begat the Steinkirk cravat, a particularly nonchalant way of fastening the cravat through a buttonhole, said to originate on the battlefield where soldiers had no time for tying. Around this time, the cravat grew to such proportions that playwright William Congreve dismissed it as a 'slabbering bib' in his comedy *Love for Love*, which premiered in 1695.[51]

Just as Gundulić's cravat had spread via the military, Central and Eastern European mercenaries continued to exert influence on the fashionable dress of both men and women. Starting in the 15th century, Hungarian Hussar regiments joined many European armies and, over the following centuries, spread their distinctive uniforms throughout the continent. The key feature of the Hussar jacket was elaborate ornamental frogging, likely inspired by the decoration on Ottoman Turkish kaftans (*see* page 74).[52] During the Napoleonic wars of the early 19th century, Hussars in the French army sparked women's trends for cropped spencer jackets, long coats known as redingotes and dresses *à la Hussar*.[53] The style has remained famous in more recent years, thanks to its association with music stars Jimi Hendrix and Adam Ant.

Hailing from a powerful Florentine banking and political dynasty, Marie de' Medici became Queen of France after marrying King Henry IV, the first French king from the House of Bourbon. Marie had a turbulent time in France: her husband was assassinated; she quarrelled with her son Louis XIII and was exiled; and, after reconciling with her son, she left France again following a conflict with Cardinal Richelieu. However, her hold on fashion has been much more stable.

Both Marie and her distant relation Catherine de' Medici (who was Queen of France earlier in the 16th century) have been credited with introducing to the French court different styles of ruff made of Venetian lace.[34] Most portraits of Marie show her in a standing lace collar, rather than a cartwheel ruff that went all the way around the neck.

Marie de' Medici
c.1575–1642

The ruff is an icon of 16th-century dress. Starched and kept in place by a structure known as a supportasse or piccadill, a standing ruff was a marker of wealth and status, not only due to the expense of lace, but also because it was incredibly labour-intensive to launder, and had to be restarched and reshaped with hot irons for each wearing. When costume designers re-created authentic ruffs for a production at the Globe Theatre, they found it took more than three hours to set one neck and two wrist ruffs.[55] Moralists in England maligned the size and audacity of ruffs, and puritanical pamphleteer Philip Stubbes decried starch as the devil's liquor when it was introduced from the Netherlands in the 1560s.[56]

From at least the 1830s onwards, the style of ruff worn by Marie de' Medici took on her name in the fashion press. In 1830 and 1831, British magazine *La Belle Assemblée* presented outfits that included 'a large collar turned back, and cut in long and very sharp points *à la Medicis*,'[57] a collar 'partially turned up in the Medicis style'[58] and a walking dress of 'cambric chemisette, with a ruff of the same material, *à la Marie Medicis*.'[59] Nearly a century later in 1922, American *Vogue* ran a feature on fashion at the time of Henry IV and Marie, with the collar as a standout feature. 'Of lace was made one of Marie de Medici's few permanent contributions to the mode, the fan-like collar which has come down to us bearing her name, and which is seldom out of fashion.'[60]

Moralists in England maligned the size and audacity of ruffs, and puritanical pamphleteer Philip Stubbes decried starch as the devil's liquor when it was introduced from the Netherlands in the 1560s.

ANN ZINGHA,

Queen of Matamba.

*The original of this picture, painted on parchment, is to be found in Portugal
in a convent of Coimbra.*

London published by Bull & Churton, 26, Holles St. Cavendish Square.

Throughout much of the first half of the 17th century, Queen Nzinga was ruler of the Mbundu people in Ndongo and Matamba in present-day Angola. This was a pivotal time in the history of the region, as Portuguese traders were attempting to infiltrate the coast of West and Central Africa to establish colonies and increase trade. Demand for slave labour from Africa was growing in European colonies in North and South America as slave-harvested sugar, and later cotton, became vastly profitable commodities. Today, Nzinga is celebrated as a folk hero for her part in resisting Portuguese rule and maintaining independence. Throughout her lifetime she was forced to make morally complex diplomatic pacts, siding at times with the Portuguese and later with the Dutch (as well as selling them exports, including slaves), to remain free of colonial rule.

Queen Nzinga
of Ndongo & Matamba
1583–1663

Recent biographers have noted Nzinga's use of clothing in her diplomatic relations. It is claimed that while she had access to European imports later in life, she wore Mbundu styles rather than European fashions in Luanda, the key destination for trade with the Portuguese. These included 'priceless jewels' and 'coloured feathers'[61] in her hair. She adorned her hands, feet and legs with rings made of iron, copper, gold, silver, coral and glass, which highlighted her royal status and offered talismanic protection from illness and physical harm. She was buried with an array of her favourite items, from silk laces trimmed with gold to royal crowns.[62]

Nzinga converted to Christianity and was baptized, but sources from the time, largely Capuchin missionaries, emphasized her 'barbarism' by stating that she dressed as a man and demanded to be called King rather than Queen. A Dutch captain wrote that she 'dressed in man's apparel... hanging about her the skin of beasts... with a Sword about her neck, an Axe at her girdle, and a Bow and Arrows in her hand.'[63] Most enslaved people from present-day Angola were sent by the Portuguese to Brazil, where Nzinga's memory is kept alive through traditions and celebrations such as the symbolic crowning of the King of the Kongo and Queen Nzinga on church feast days.[64]

Shah Jahan (born Shahab-ud-din Muhammad Khurram) reigned from 1628 to 1658 as the fifth Mughal emperor. The Mughal Empire in the Indian subcontinent was established in 1526 and ruled by a Muslim dynasty from Central Asia. Shah Jahan is known for his architectural legacy, primarily the Taj Mahal, the mausoleum

Shah Jahan
1592—1666

he built in Agra for his wife Mumtaz Mahal who died in childbirth in 1631. The Mughal emperors were known for their devotion to luxury. Shah Jahan's father and the previous emperor, Jahangir, was described by the English ambassador in 1616, as 'covered in huge pearls, diamonds and rubies as large as walnuts...and wore a coat of cloth of gold'[65]

Cotton is native to the Indus Valley and had been traded in the region for centuries. During the reign of Shah Jahan and his successor, his third son Aurangzeb, commerce with Western Europe flourished, a trade that revolutionized the way Western Europeans dressed. In 1600 the East India Company was granted a Royal Charter from Elizabeth I and soon began to import cotton goods. Before this time, the majority of the population dressed in wool and linen, or a mix of the two known as fustian. The rich added silk to this list. Cotton was much lighter, more comfortable and much easier to wash than wool. It was cheaper than silk, and could be printed or painted with colourfast dyes to create chintz. Dye techniques were sophisticated in India, resulting in an intensity and longevity of colour that was unknown in much of Europe, and was more cost-effective than embroidered or woven decoration. The East India Company sent instructions to India to modify designs for the English market, in part based on the vogue for chinoiserie. Originally used for furnishings such as curtains or bed hangings, chintz soon crossed into the fashionable wardrobe. By the 1660s, textiles made up nearly three-quarters of the export trade from India.[66]

Shah Jahan was not as clothes-oriented as his forebears but his rule laid the groundwork for Indian textiles to become the height of fashion in Western Europe. Chintz was soon regarded as a defining marker of English country style, and the desire to replicate colourful, affordable Indian cottons for the European market became one of the key drivers of the Industrial Revolution in Britain.

In 1660 Charles II was reinstated on the English throne, 11 years after his father had been beheaded. His reign saw not only the return of the monarchy, but also a new style of dress for men that broke with the doublet and hose in favour of a new, more streamlined silhouette that has been hailed as the forerunner to the modern three-piece suit.

On 8 October 1666, Samuel Pepys wrote in his diary: 'The King hath yesterday in Council declared his resolution of setting a fashion for clothes, which he will never alter. It will be a vest, I know not well how; but it is to teach the nobility thrift, and will do good.' The vest had long sleeves and was cut close to the body, reaching halfway to the knees. Just nine days later Pepys commented: 'The Court is all full of vests.' Orders for the vest can be seen in the king's wardrobe accounts, held at the National Archives in London, and show that the last requests for the vest came just four years later.

Charles II, nicknamed the 'Merry Monarch', walked a fine line between dressing in a regal manner fit for a king and avoiding the extravagance of his father. Between 1666 and 1667, France and England were briefly at war. Adopting the vest was propaganda: Charles was outwardly distancing himself from the thrall of his cousin Louis XIV at the French court, where he had spent time in exile, and at the same time he was advocating restraint in dress to dissociate himself from the profligacy of his father. Somewhat ironically, French tailor Claude Sourceau, who first worked for the king when he was in exile and continued after the Restoration alongside John Allen, created Charles's new English vest.[67]

As with all monarchs, clothing played a political role. The king remained cognizant of the importance of appearing to favour English dress, and his wardrobe was full of English wools. His father's wardrobe accounts, in contrast, noted bright satins in colours such as carnation, primrose, grass green and lemon.[68] Charles II issued a proclamation in the 1670s that he would, 'henceforth wear none but English manufactures except linen and calico', and that no one wearing foreign lace could appear in his presence.[69] The vest may have been short-lived, but the change to menswear was long-lasting.

King Charles II of England, Scotland & Ireland

1630–85

Swedish Queen Christina became queen elect in 1632 and was made queen in 1644, later abdicating to convert to Catholicism in 1654. Under her father's orders she was educated as a prince and, due to a quirk of Swedish law that did not allow a woman to hold power, was crowned king. After abdicating, she became a patron of the arts across Europe and advocated religious tolerance in a period defined by holy war. She has lived on in culture as the subject of numerous plays, films and other works of art. In the 20th century she became a feminist figure for her independence and androgyny, as well as an icon in LGBT+ history, in part due to her clothing.[70]

Queen Christina Vasa of Sweden
1626–89

Biographers claim that, after abdicating, Christina left Sweden disguised as a knight, in male accoutrements such as high boots and with a sword at her side.[71] Accounts of the time note 'masculine' attributes, as outlined in 1656: 'Her bodice is tied so tightly in the back that it looks like a man's doublet…she wears men's shoes, and her voice and manner are very masculine.'[72] In an era when power and patronage were almost exclusively male, Christina did not fit comfortably into 17th-century notions of femininity[73]

Queen Christina's wardrobe continued to have an impact centuries later. In 1933 MGM released a biopic of the Swedish monarch, starring Greta Garbo, Swedish queen of the silver screen. Her biography was changed to a conventional love story, but hints at subversion appeared, including male clothing (costumed by Adrian) and a lingering kiss between Garbo and her lady-in-waiting. Macy's Cinema Shop sold a selection of garments adapted from the film, and the impact of the costumes on fashion was evident in the trade press for more than a year after the release. Articles noted the gender ambiguity of the queen's wardrobe: 'A paradoxical silhouette – as alluringly feminine and forthrightly boyish as the paradoxical Queen Christina herself'.[74] Despite the adoption of trousers by stars such as Garbo and Marlene Dietrich at this time, the styles copied were predominantly dresses.

Thirty-five years after Hollywood immortalized her, Queen Christina featured on the pages of *Vogue*, in an editorial starring model Veruschka wearing 'clothes of 17th-century romanticism: rich velvets, falls of clean white linen and lace – all intensely, vividly wearable now'.[75] Queen Christina remains an icon whose style is paradoxically sold as being modern in its historicism.

Thirty-five years after Hollywood immortalized her, Queen Christina featured on the pages of *Vogue*.

Louis XIV is a force to be contended with in the history of fashion, power and style. Just four years old when he inherited the French crown, he went on to reign for 72 years. His championing of the fashion industry ensured France became the arbiter of style and taste that it remains today. Louis understood the idea of power through spectacle and, along with Jean-Baptiste Colbert, the Minister of Finance, he recognized the potential of fashion and luxury goods for the French economy. Colbert organized trade guilds to regulate the industry and noted: 'Fashion is to France what the gold mines of Peru are to Spain.'[76] The importance of the fashion industry for the country's coffers was noted by the English writer and diarist John Evelyn who stated in his tract *Tyrannus or the Mode* (1661), that in France, fashion 'feeds as many bellies as it clothes backs'.

King Louis XIV of France

1638–1715

'Fashion is to France what the gold mines of Peru are to Spain.'

Shrewd moves between Louis and Colbert put France's fashion industry on the global stage. They outlawed the importing of foreign cloth and trimmings, ensuring the silk industry around Lyons flourished due to royal patronage, especially after the epicentre moved to the Palace of Versailles in 1682. Life at Versailles was a highly ritualized theatre of power and control. As an anointed monarch, the king's dressing and undressing (*lever* and *coucher*) were partially public events that provided crucial moments of contact – and possible influence – between him and favoured courtiers. Louis's insistence on finery at court and his encouragement of a culture of competitive ostentation left many of his courtiers in debt. The king often settled these debts himself, guaranteeing him loyalty from his nobles.

Fashion was used as a means of distinction, to visually indicate status and the rule of an absolute monarch. A particular favourite of his were red high heels, which showed off his dancer's legs to advantage. Fashion became an area of overwhelming importance, and at one point around one-third of wage earners in Paris were employed in some capacity by the industry.[77] It was also under the reign of Louis XIV that the precursor of the modern-day fashion shoot originated, in a 1678 supplement to the magazine *Le Nouveau Mercure Galant* that featured full-length illustrations of a man and a woman, annotated with supplier details.[78] So began the reign of Paris as the centre of the fashion world, a reign that has outlived the French monarchy itself.

Writer and poet, Lady Mary Wortley Montagu travelled widely, but is best known for the letters she wrote from the Ottoman Empire as wife to the British ambassador to Turkey from 1717 to 1718. Manuscripts of the letters were circulated in her lifetime and published posthumously. Montagu brought a number of ideas to England from Turkey, including variolation, an early form of smallpox inoculation. It failed to catch on widely until Edward Jenner proposed a similar but safer method later in the century.

In her letters Montagu outlined her adoption of Ottoman dress in detail. On her return to England, she was painted a number of times in the clothing she brought back, as well as in westernized versions of the styles. The items she described were staples of Ottoman women's clothing: 'The first piece of my dress is a pair of drawers [*şalvar*], very full, that reach to my shoes and conceal the legs more modestly than your petticoats. They are of a thin rose colour damask brocaded with silver flowers.'[79] She noted items such as the chemise or smock (*gömlek*), robe (*entari*) and kaftan. That drawers were seen to offer more freedom of movement is evident in the adoption of this element of 'Turkish dress' by Amelia Bloomer (*see* page 134) and other dress reformers in the following century.

The covert attack on rules of modesty in Western Europe is a running theme throughout Montagu's letters that debate ideas around freedom and dress. She discusses the independence and anonymity of veiling: ''Tis very easy to see they have more Liberty than we have…no Man dare either touch or follow a Woman in the Street'.[80] And she ponders the caging of corsetry in Western European fashions that prohibit her from undressing at the public baths.[81]

Montagu's letters heightened the growing trend for dressing *à la Turque* in fashionable dress, portraiture and masquerade costume. Diplomatic visits fanned the flames of Turquerie in France, and the influential Madame de Pompadour, chief mistress of King Louis XV, commissioned Turkish-style interiors and paintings in the middle of the century.[82] 'Turkomania', including turbans, kaftans and fur-trimmed robes, crossed the Atlantic on the publication of Montagu's letters in the American colonies in the 1760s. They remained a popular source of inspiration throughout the century, and were serialized in the first issues of *The Ladies' Magazine* in the 1790s.[83]

Lady Mary Wortley Montagu
1689–1762

Late Modern

mid 18th–19th Century

In 1644 the Qing dynasty came to power, the last empire in Chinese history, and governed until it was overthrown in the Revolution of 1911. It was ruled by the Manchus, a nomadic group that came from the north. Much of what we know today as Chinese material culture developed during this period, including clothing. Manchu rulers were keen to keep their ethnic identity distinct from the Han Chinese, yet they integrated features of previous Ming dynasty robes into the Manchu imperial regalia. These features signalled the equestrian nature of their nomadic heritage, such as horseshoe-shaped cuffs that were better suited to riding.[1]

Qianlong Emperor
1711–99

Qianlong Emperor increased the size of his vast Chinese kingdom to create a multi-ethnic empire during his long reign from 1735 to 1796. By all accounts, he was highly cultured and had a passionate interest in curating and collecting art and antiquities for the imperial collection at the Forbidden City.[2] His enthusiasm extended to documenting imperial court dress in 1759. Formal wear was divided into five categories for state functions: official, festive, regular, travelling and military. Silk was the favoured fabric, and its importance was commemorated through offerings at the Altar of the Silkworms. Weaving was traditionally a woman's job, so the empress performed the ritual.[3]

In many premodern societies across the globe, the idea prevailed that the structure of society should be enshrined in dress codes, and often in law. In China, the philosophical and political text *Guanzi*, dating from the 7th century BCE, noted: 'Let no one, even if worthy and honored, dare wear clothing that does not befit his rank.'[4] This continued under Qianlong Emperor, especially regarding the imperial colour yellow, which was reserved for the royal household in various hues: bright yellow for the emperor, his mother, empress and first concubine; apricot yellow for his heir; and golden yellow for his other sons. The 'Twelve Symbols' were also reserved for the emperor alone, and traced their lineage back to the previous dynasty and earlier. The emperor cut quite a dash in his imperial robes, as described by a British valet at the Qing court in 1793: 'His dress consisted of a loose robe of yellow silk, a cap of black velvet with a red ball on the top, and adorned with a peacock's feather.'[5]

Giacomo Casanova
1725–98

Casanova's name has become a byword for sexual excess, largely due to his autobiography, *Histoire de ma vie*, which documents his escapades and numerous romantic liaisons. He travelled extensively in Europe and met influential figures, from Catherine the Great (*see* page 115) to Voltaire and Mozart, providing a colourful account of bohemian peripatetic 18th-century life and society.

Casanova was born in the Republic of Venice. His mother was an actress, and so his is a story of social mobility born of life on the theatrical margins. An exploration of the idiosyncrasies of the Venetian city-state in the 18th century helps us to understand Casanova's life, even though he spent such a great part of it travelling.

During the 18th century Venice became a tourist destination, thanks to the carnival, with pleasure seekers visiting for the transgressive thrill of masked anonymity and the mix of social classes. Venice was transformed into a playground, with actors, acrobats, street performers, musicians, street vendors and wild animals competing for attention. In the early 1720s a visitor wrote: 'As the *Carnival* advances, the Dress grows more various and whimsical: the Women make themselves Nymphs and Shepherdesses, the men Scaramouches and Punchinellos...For further Variety, they sometimes change Sexes: Women appear in Men's Habits, and Men in Women's.'[6]

The use of masks in Venice dates back to the 13th century, and possibly (but not definitively) comes from the sacking and defeat of Constantinople by Venetian command in 1204. This provided access to rare commodities from the Middle and Far East, which may have included masks. However, from the 1690s until the fall of the Republic in 1797, mask-wearing was part of daily life, not only during carnival, but also for about six months of the year from autumn until Lent.

Standard garb for 18th-century men and women maskers was the *tabàro*, a black cloak and hood that hid the neck and encircled the face. This was worn with a three-cornered hat and the white mask known today as the *baùta*. If hatless, women could wear the *morèta* mask of lace or velvet that was held in place by a small button clenched between the teeth.[7]

Venice formed the backdrop to Casanova's early life, but throughout his travels he attended Venetian-style masked balls in cities from London to St Petersburg. As one biographer noted: 'It is impossible to overestimate the fashionability of Venice and Venetians in Casanova's lifetime.'[8]

Catherine the Great
1729—96

Empress Catherine II of Russia was born Sophie of Anhalt-Zerbst, a Prussian princess. She married into the ruling Romanov dynasty, and came to power after a coup d'état that saw her husband Tsar Peter III assassinated. Catherine II ruled for 34 years, and her life has been shrouded in speculation and rumour regarding her lovers and favourites. She was an autocratic ruler, but reformed and modernized Russian society and expanded education for girls in institutes for schooling that were unparalleled at the time. A patron of the arts, her extensive collection formed the basis of the Hermitage Museum.

Peter the Great, Catherine II's grandfather-in-law, irretrievably altered Russian dress. In 1701 he decreed that the aristocracy and townspeople of Russia must wear European fashions. Prior to this declaration, Muscovite dress had reflected the ethnic and cultural diversity of the region, from the nomadic Tatar people in the north to the Slavic and Finnish groups across the Russian heartland. Clothes had tended to be flowing and loose, rather than the more tailored European styles that Peter introduced.[9] The edict came with the penalty of a fine or expulsion from court if ignored, with the only exclusions being peasants and Orthodox clergy. As an incentive and means to advance local industry, Peter wore European fashions made only of Russian textiles.[10] This move marked a schism in dress between 'traditional' Russian styles and European elite fashion. To showcase modernized European design, Peter had a new capital city constructed: St Petersburg became known as the 'Venice of the North'.

Catherine II sent many messages about her rule and patronage of Russian customs and culture through her own dress, incorporating, for example, elements of Russian military uniform into her own clothing.[11] During her reign, amid growing Russian national consciousness, Catherine attempted to reintroduce traditional elements into women's dress by declaring what should be worn at court. This was based on the *sarafan*, a sleeveless dress often decorated with floral silk-brocade ribbons, and the headdress called the *kokoshnik*.[12] Even before this declaration, Russian decorative features such as floral embroidery and lace trimmings had been mixed with the European fashions worn at court.[13] The reintroduction of traditional items was also intended to curb the outrageous spending on fashions, yet a foreign chronicler noted Catherine's own costume was 'covered with diamonds' at a ball.[14]

The last Queen of France before the revolution, Marie Antoinette was certainly a victim of her love for fashion. Forever associated in the popular imagination with *ancien-régime* (old-order) excess and opulence, she was given the nickname 'Madame Déficit' for her love of spending. The queen broke with etiquette through her patronage of *marchande de mode* (fashion merchant) Rose Bertin, rather than using private court dressmakers. Access to the queen was a crucial part of the power play of court life at Versailles, and to allow a non-noble merchant such unprecedented access succeeded in alienating many courtiers.[15]

Marie Antoinette
1755—93

Marie Antoinette's most salacious fashion transgression was an ensemble that became known as the *chemise à la reine* or the *gaulle*. Conventional court dress was the *grand habit*, a formal ensemble that was restrictive and cumbersome to wear. Marie Antoinette bucked convention at the Petit Trianon, her country retreat in the grounds of the Palace of Versailles. By 1780 one of her favourite styles was the *gaulle*, a white muslin gown that was drawn over the head and tied with a sash, and had originated on the plantations of the French West Indies.[16] It was this that she chose to wear for a portrait displayed at the Louvre. The painting caused such controversy that it was hastily removed and the artist Élisabeth Vigée-Lebrun painted another more suitable picture. The informal layers of muslin were much too relaxed for a portrait of a queen, and it quickly garnered the moniker *chemise à la reine*. A *chemise* being the bottom layer worn against the skin, the name implied that the queen had been painted in her underwear. She was also accused of putting French silk weavers out of business by favouring cotton. The moment was significant in turning public opinion against the monarchy, and by the end of the decade the country was in the midst of a revolution. The queen saved her final white *chemise* in her prison cell to ride to the guillotine in 1793.[17]

Perhaps unsurprisingly, the *chemise à la reine* remained popular post-revolution as a much more egalitarian style. The earliest years of the 19th century were defined by simple white dresses featuring the high-waist Empire line. Empress Joséphine, Napoleon's first wife, was even a fan of the style: in the inventory after her death in 1814, 529 out of her 751 dresses were made from muslin or other cotton fabrics.[18]

The inimitable Duchess of Devonshire reigned over London high society in the late 18th century. She married the Duke of Devonshire in 1774, and the couple split their time between Devonshire House in London and the grand Chatsworth House estate in Derbyshire. A supporter (and sometime canvasser) for the Whig political party, Georgiana wielded considerable influence in unofficial social politics.

Georgiana's wit and sartorial verve ensured she was feted as a society beauty. She regularly topped newspaper polls of fashionable women, including *The Morning Post*'s 'Scale of Bon Ton' and *London Chronicle*'s 'Scale of Beauties' in 1776, when London's most sought-after hostesses were graded according to qualities such as elegance, grace and principles.[19] Her lifestyle matched her social brilliance, with a coterie of fashionable friends ranging from Marie Antoinette (*see* page 116) to Beau Brummell (*see* page 126). A considerable taste for luxury, plus her love of gambling, led to heavy debts throughout her life. Georgiana was known for her flamboyance, which could be the subject of satire and ridicule. As a fashion leader she set a number of trends, from 90-cm (3-foot) hair towers padded with horsehair and adorned with ornaments to the drooping ostrich feather arranged across the front of the head. Rare and expensive, these newly popular plumes were criticized for being too excessive and were eventually banned from court by the queen.[20] After the scandal of giving birth to an illegitimate child, she was chastised by her mother, who drew on the age-old correlation between morality and appearance: 'I am sure I need not warn you to observe the strictest sobriety and moderation in your dress...and how glad I should be if you could tell me you had quite done with rouge.'[21]

Georgiana's lasting stylistic legacy was the 'picture hat', captured in a portrait by Thomas Gainsborough in the mid-1780s (*see* opposite). Designed by her, the dramatic oversized black hat was trimmed with a sash and her signature drooping feathers, and worn at a rakish angle. After the painting was put on display, women across the country copied the style.[22] Georgiana's taste for theatrical millinery echoes through the centuries, with American *Vogue* announcing in 1923: 'The uncurled ostrich feather has been restored to its proud place...posed at the side front of a hat, which Gainsborough might have painted.'[23]

Georgiana Cavendish,
Duchess of Devonshire
1757–1806

Fashion and dress took on hugely ideological roles during the French Revolution. Radical journalist Jacques Hébert founded and edited the newspaper *Le Père Duchesne* during crucial years of the revolutionary movement, including the Reign of Terror when many thousands were executed due to real or imagined disloyalty to the revolutionary cause. To convey its populist message, the newspaper was based on Père Duchesne, a folkloric character who represented a man of the people. Hébert often used obscenity and heightened emotion, and Marie Antoinette was a regular target.

Jacques Hébert
1757–94

The *sans-culottes* ('without knee breeches') faction of the French Revolution is one of history's clearest examples of using clothing and its symbolism to establish a collective political identity and ideological function. It was this group that Hébert's newspaper represented. There is much historical debate about the make-up of the *sans-culottes*.[24] but as a marker of popular working-class revolutionary zeal they became recognizable in prints and pamphlets for their dress: trousers instead of knee breeches, a short jacket (*carmagnole*) and a woollen cap (*bonnet rouge* or liberty cap).[25] Historically, working men wore loose trousers, while wealthier men of fashion wore knee breeches and silk stockings. This was largely a question of practicality as working men needed more ease of movement, and it became a clear symbol of class divide, as romanticized in a portrait by Louis-Léopold Boilly (*see* opposite).

In the paranoid atmosphere of the Reign of Terror, all dress codes became ideologically loaded with the potential to be dissected by public censure. Hébert's journal *Le Père Duchesne* had pointed out earlier the heightened symbolism that dress could take on, saying, 'if an apron was a rallying sign, it would be necessary to prevent even cooks from wearing them'.[26] Hébert himself succumbed to the revolutionary mob in 1794. His executioner reportedly waved a *bonnet rouge* in his face before he died.[27]

By the end of the 1790s, the *sans-culotte* dress code had largely been abandoned[28] but the impact on fashion remained. Fashion magazines were revived in 1797 with the publication of *Journal des Dames et des Modes*, which pronounced that loose clothing was too 'peasant-like' to be considered fashion. However, just two years later the same magazine asserted that knee breeches were only seen at balls and that pantaloons (the more egalitarian option) were instead the articles of choice for everyday wear.[29]

'Oh! what a tangled web we weave,' wrote Walter Scott in his 1808 poem *Marmion: A Tale of Flodden Field*. No web was so tangled as Scott's place in reinventing the history of tartan and Scottish national dress. There has been a great deal of historical debate over the origins of tartan and key emblems of Scottish dress such as the kilt,[30] but the backstory to Scott's involvement started in 1746, following the Battle of Culloden between England and Scotland. An act of parliament outlawed the wearing of tartan, kilts and 'highland garb' with a penalty of six months in prison, or overseas transportation for a second offence. During the ban, the Highland regiments of the British army – clad in Black Watch tartan uniforms – helped to keep tradition alive, and, finally, the act was repealed in 1782, thanks to the assistance of the Highland Society of London.

Sir Walter Scott
1771—1832

In 1822, poet and novelist Walter Scott, keen tartan enthusiast and president of the Celtic Society of Edinburgh, was tasked with stage-managing the visit of George IV to Scotland (*see* portrait overleaf), the first visit of a reigning monarch in nearly two hundred years. The resulting pageant was an extravaganza of Highland accoutrements, and the ensuing vogue for tartan, which was even donned by the king, saw manufacturers such as William Wilson & Son of Bannockburn develop a number of certified 'clan tartans' in its wake.[31] Scott had successfully restored tartan and items such as the kilt as part of the establishment and a popular display of Scottish national identity.[32]

The royal endorsement continued after Queen Victoria leased Balmoral in 1848, and used red Royal Stewart, green Hunting Stewart and white Dress Stewart tartans for upholstery, curtains and carpets.[33] Through trade, migration and slavery, tartan also has links around the world, from India to Japan and the African diaspora.[34] Vivienne Westwood added to the story when she repurposed tartan for her early punk designs, infusing it with an element of anti-establishment rebellion. Alexander McQueen, drawing on his own Scottish heritage, revisited the Battle of Culloden in his collections 'Highland Rape' (Autumn/Winter 1995-6) and 'Widows of Culloden' (Autumn/Winter 2006-7). He even created his own McQueen tartan in red, yellow and black. The Scottish Register of Tartans today verifies and registers new tartan designs from all over the world, a fitting legacy for Sir Walter Scott.

Walter Scott was tasked with stage–managing the visit of George IV to Scotland... The resulting pageant was an extravaganza of Highland accoutrements.

In the early 19th century a new breed of sartorially conscious young men known as the Dandies dominated the streets and soirées of the West End of London. Their leader was George Bryan 'Beau' Brummell, the son of a civil servant who became friends with the Prince of Wales (later King George IV). Brummell was raised as a gentleman and the clothing he wore both at Eton College and in the 10th Light Dragoons, a cavalry regiment of the British army, informed his taste in dress.

George Bryan 'Beau' Brummell

1778–1840

When Beau came of age in 1799, one-third of the family estate was released to him. His first purchases were the best wardrobe in the West End and a residence that would act as a theatre for his vestimentary obsessions.[35] Crowds of men arrived at Brummell's residence each morning in the hope of watching him dress. As an early biographer wrote: 'his first great innovation was effected upon neckcloths',[36] and, aided by his valet, Brummell could easily discard a number of cravats before achieving the desired effect.

men only

JULY
1950

PRICE

1/6
NET

BEAU BRUMMEL

Hynes.

The term 'dandy' has metamorphosed in current usage to mean a particularly flashy, flamboyant style of dress. Yet Brummell's style was the exact opposite: minimalist by standards of the time, with a restricted colour palette of blue-black, white and buff. Brummell was not only fastidious about his dress, but also about hygiene. He bathed every day (an anomaly at the time) and his mantra – 'No perfumes, but fine linen, plenty of it, and country washing' – alluded to how often he changed his linen underclothing, which he sent out of London to be cleaned away from city grime.

A man of expensive tastes, Brummell lived beyond his means and was exiled to France in the 1820s to avoid his creditors.[37] However, he successfully popularized a new masculine silhouette that focused less on showy fabrics, such as ornate brocades, and more on the lines of classical statues, like those being excavated across Europe at the time. New tailors and outfitters sprang up in the wake of his influence, and the ensuing trend for pared-down, tailored menswear saw the shopping geography of the West End expand and adapt to meet the growing demands of stylish young men, a legacy that can still be felt around Mayfair's Savile Row.

Labelled 'mad, bad and dangerous to know' by Lady Caroline Lamb with whom he had an affair, George Gordon Byron was the quintessential Romantic poet. His numerous scandals, literary success and artfully dishevelled appearance combined to form the image of the 'Byronic hero' in his poetry as well as in his life. Often cited as an early example of a celebrity, he quipped to a friend on the publication of his narrative poem *Childe Harold's Pilgrimage* in 1812: 'I awoke one morning and found myself famous.'[38]

Lord Byron
1788–1824

Byron understood the power of fame at a moment when image reproduction was getting easier and cheaper due to improvements in printing technology.[39] In cultivating his 'Byronic' persona, he attempted to control the circulation and construction of his likeness. His *déshabillé* appearance confirmed his image as a melancholy yet passionate, tortured poet. A sweeping black cloak, wild dark hair and, crucially, the loose, open collar are synonymous with his role: an outward manifestation of inner turmoil.

His *déshabillé* appearance confirmed his image as a melancholy yet passionate, tortured poet.

R. Westall, R.A. pinxt.   T. Illman, sculpt.

GEORGE GORDON, LORD

It has been suggested that his stylized look was not authentic, rather an artistic affectation that differed from his more conventional daily dress. Financial accounts indicate that he spent substantial sums on fine Irish linen and French cambric for his undershirts,[40] but an article in the *Literary Gazette* four years after he died questioned the accuracy of his daring neckline: 'From his portraits it has been supposed that he wore no cravat, but went with his neck open – which was not the case. He used to wear a small cravat with the collar turned down; but always sat for his likeness without one.'[41]

A biographer of Byron's contemporary Beau Brummell (*see* page 126) claimed that early portraits of Byron were overpainted to show an open shirt, where a fashionable neckcloth had once been.[42] Regardless of its authenticity, his look was influential. It appeared in shop windows and he arguably played a considerable part in popularizing black for menswear, especially in evening dress.[43]

The other (in)famous image of Byron, painted by Thomas Phillips in 1813, shows the poet in Albanian dress, which he acquired on his Grand Tour of the Mediterranean in 1809 (*see* opposite). With a draped turban and gold-embroidered jacket, he exhibits himself as a cosmopolitan man of action. This image was one he cultivated in life as well as art, as he died of fever having travelled to Missolonghi to fight for Greek independence from the Ottoman Empire. In the 1960s, dress historian Doris Langley Moore rediscovered the Albanian ensemble when she was collecting pieces for her newly inaugurated Museum of Costume in Bath, and it can still be found in the collection at Bowood House, Wiltshire.[44]

Amelia Bloomer was a temperance supporter and women's rights activist, who leant her name to the undergarment known as bloomers. The 'bloomer costume' consisted of baggy 'Turkish' pantaloon-style trousers that reached the ankle and an overskirt that finished 10cm (4 inches) below the knee. This eponymous hero of bloomers was not their first advocate – this was Elizabeth Smith Miller – yet it was Bloomer's championing through her newspaper *The Lily* that saw them spread to international prominence.

Many patrons of the women's movement praised this style of dress for being practical and sanitary. Bloomer claimed that as soon as the 'Turkish style' was publicized, she was inundated with requests for patterns so women could make their own, which in her words showed 'how ready and anxious women were to throw off the burden of long, heavy skirts'.[45] Bloomers enthusiasts were spotted handing out leaflets for dress-reform lectures at the UK's Great Exhibition of 1851, and, in the same year, a New York paper reported on a '"Bloomer Ball" at which the attendees were gaudily attired'.[46]

The 'Bloomerism' movement met with censure in the press on both sides of the Atlantic. Bifurcated clothing on women was a visual manifestation of gender disruption, a visceral metaphor of society being turned on its head. *Punch* magazine published numerous cartoons lampooning the style (and the aims of the women involved), while women's publication *Peterson's Magazine* claimed that women lost their 'natural grace' when attired like a man. Other magazines worried that accessories such as canes and cigars might come next.[47] *The New York Times* took a more severe approach, noting in 1852: 'These ladies assert their claim to rights, which we of bifurcated raiment are charged with usurping. This claim conflicts with, and if secured, will tend to diminish the rights of masculine mankind.'[48]

It was partly due to this distracting sartorial criticism that Bloomer and her fellow campaigners renounced their style of dress. Bloomer adopted the cage crinoline when it was introduced, which was much lighter and less restrictive than layers of heavy petticoats. She later wrote: 'We all felt that the dress was drawing attention from what we thought of far greater importance – the question of woman's right to better education, to a wider field of employment, to better remuneration for her labour, and to the ballot for the protection of her rights.'[49]

Amelia Bloomer
1818–94

Amalia of Oldenburg

1818–75

Greek independence was won from the Ottoman Empire in a war that lasted from 1821 to 1832. The aftermath of the complicated conflict saw three of the Great Powers, France, Britain and Russia, claim a stake in the politics of the new nation, deciding that the Greek state would be ruled by a Bavarian prince, Otto von Wittelsbach, who duly became King of Greece in 1832. In 1836 Otto married Duchess Amalia Maria Frederica of Oldenburg, who returned to Greece with him the following year as his queen.

With this convoluted political backdrop, it is understandable that the new king and queen wanted to legitimize their reign through various means, one of which was dress. Otto adopted a wide-sleeved shirt and the *fustanella*, a multi-gored skirt made of cotton or linen. The *fustanella* probably originated in Albania, and was crystalized as Greek dress during and in the aftermath of the War of Independence, as a show of gratitude to Albanian fighters. Otto cemented its position when he made it formal court clothing.[50] A version survives in the uniform of the Greek Presidential Guard.

Amalia introduced a part-Greek, part-Viennese ensemble that became known as the Amalia Costume. It consisted of a long dress with wide skirts, as was popular in Western Europe at the time, with elaborate embroidery on the chemise beneath the bodice; a cropped velvet jacket, often red and embroidered with gold; and a red brimless cap with a long gold tassel. The distinctive jacket, known as a *kondogouni* or *zipouni*, also came in black or blue, and was embroidered by tailors called *terzides*, who specialized in working with gold thread.[51]

The creation of national dress was not only a Greek phenomenon in the 19th century. With the unification of countries and the creation of nation-states, there was a strong desire to forge a national identity through dress in many regions. The romanticization of rural life in the wake of the Industrial Revolution and a desire for tradition in the face of encroaching modernity also explain the prominence given to folk styles in these designs. Even though Otto and Amalia were expelled from Greece after an uprising in 1862, variations on the Amalia Costume and the *fustanella* are still seen on Greek national holidays.

An Italian general and politician, Giuseppe Garibaldi played a leading role in the unification of Italy and the establishment of the Italian nation-state. He landed in Sicily in 1860 with an army of volunteers that he had inspired to take up arms. This shifted the balance of power away from the aristocracy and encouraged the new social order of the Risorgimento (unification). Described as an international freedom fighter (which led to global fame), he came to embody the myth of the archetypal selfless moral hero, a man whom British historian A J P Taylor identified as the 'only wholly admirable figure in modern history'.[52]

reminiscent of romanticized peasant or worker's styles. While red was associated with army uniforms in Europe, wearing a shirt without an overcoat or jacket was unusual.

Fashion can exist at the intersection of revolutionary politics and consumer culture, commodifying popular movements or causes. This was the case with the Garibaldi shirt as it immediately crossed into fashionable dress. In 1861 *The Englishwoman's Domestic Magazine* stated: 'The Garibaldi shirt – an article that is now so much in favour'.[54] It soon crossed the Atlantic, where *Godey's Lady's Book* noted in an article on Parisian novelties the following year: 'Destined to produce a change amounting to a revolution in ladies' costume, is the Garibaldi shirt.. In shape and pattern it is made in the same way as a gentleman's shirt'.[55] It was subsequently reported in the American fashion press that the Garibaldi shirt developed into the shirtwaist and eventually the blouse in womenswear.[56]

Giuseppe Garibaldi
1807–82

Garibaldi wore a distinctive ensemble that included a bright red shirt, an item that his followers were encouraged to adopt to give an element of uniformity to their movement. They became known as 'Redshirts', a precursor (in name but not politics) to Fascist 'Blackshirts' and Nazi 'Brownshirts'. Garibaldi's choice of the red shirt was reported to have come from his time in South America, as a journalist of the time explained: 'Over his red shirt was thrown a [South] American poncho.. His staff wore the red blouse, and afterwards the whole Italian legion adopted that colour'.[53] The shirt was notable as it was

Military themes tend to recur in fashion during times of war. Possibly as a nod to national unity, 'Garibaldi red' enjoyed renewed popularity during World War I in both the USA and Paris.[57]

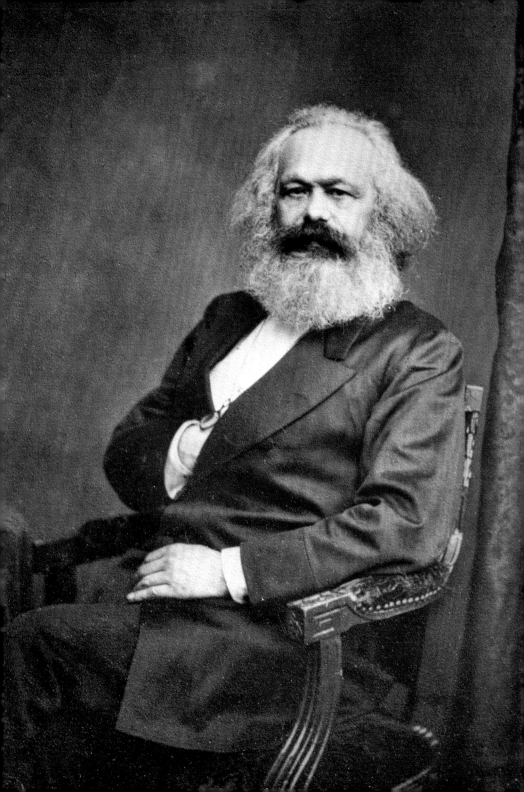

German philosopher Karl Marx would have undoubtedly eschewed the epithet 'best dressed'. Yet his theories highlight some of the problems that the fashion industry still faces. Clothing and its production were central to many of his works: 'Tailoring and weaving...are each a productive expenditure of human brains, nerves, and muscles, and in this sense are human labour', he wrote in *Capital: Critique of Political Economy* (1867).[58] He used clothing and textiles, specifically a coat and a bolt of linen, to outline his thinking about exchange values and means of production, which he believed directly contributed to the oppression of workers.

Karl Marx
1818–83

In an essay called 'Marx's Coat', the academic Peter Stallybrass reflected on clothing not only in Marx's writing but also in his lived experience. When residing in London in the 1850s and 1860s, Marx and his family survived on the small amounts of money he earned from journalism, and gifts from Friedrich Engels (his sometime collaborator who managed a Manchester cotton mill and also wrote about class struggle under industrialization). This income often fell short of their needs, and the family were regularly forced to pawn items of their clothing.

This was not an anomaly among the urban poor at this time in the UK, or among people in previous centuries. Until industrialization, clothing and textiles were often some of a family's most valuable possessions. The pawnshop was a way to temporarily recoup some of this value, in what has been called 'a banking system in clothes'.[59] However, with his overcoat pawned, Marx lacked the appearance of respectability needed to enter the Reading Rooms at the British Museum to conduct his research. As Stallybrass concludes: 'What clothes Marx wore thus shaped what he wrote.'[60]

The fashion industry is at heart a capitalist system. Obsolescence is at the core of seasonally changing fashion: we change our clothing not because it is worn out, but because it is no longer in style. This has been the basis of conspicuous fashionable display among elites for centuries. Clothing was also central to the Industrial Revolution when cotton, harvested by slave labourers on plantations in America, was converted into clothing via textile mills in the north of England. Many elements that Marx defined remain relevant today, from the separation of the means of production and consumption that led to tragedies such as the 2013 Rana Plaza factory collapse in Bangladesh, to commodity fetishism, which forms the basis of branding and the desire behind designer labels.[61]

Born in Granada, Spain, Eugénie María de Montijo de Guzmán married Emperor Napoleon III in 1853 during the Second Empire and became the last Empress of France. During this period, Paris was an imperial capital, flourishing with state balls and events. The grand redesigns of Haussmann's boulevards were the setting for a city that was yet again seen as the uncontested fashion capital of the globe, a *théâtre de la mode* of luxury goods and excessive consumption, equated with the vast cage crinolines favoured by Eugénie since their introduction in 1856. She became the figurehead of this glittering world, a fashion leader dubbed in the British press as the Queen of Fashion, Comtesse de la Crinoline, Goddess of the Bustles and Impératrice de la Mode.[62]

Empress Eugénie
1826–1920

The emphasis on dress at this time is evident from the growth of the couture industry in Paris. In 1850 there were 158 couturiers; this had risen to 1,636 by 1895.[63] This blossoming of couture is often linked to Charles Frederick Worth (1825–95), who dressed Eugénie from the early 1860s, and who styled himself as an artist–creator: the grand couturier. Originating from Lincolnshire in the UK, Worth opened 'Worth et Bobergh' in Paris with his Swedish partner in 1858. Worth was an early adopter of a number of elements that define high fashion today: the label as luxury goods branding, live models (in Worth's case, his wife Marie) and the creation of seasonal collections in line with the social calendar.

Acting as a fashion leader was not new for a European empress, but leading a nation was far more unusual. Napoleon III appointed Eugénie regent when he left to fight the Franco-Austrian War (1859), and she was involved in crucial political manoeuvres, from the question of Italian unification to governance in Mexico. Her style credentials were used to undermine her position, with her detractors claiming that the government was in the hands of 'a fashion plate'.[64] The Franco-Prussian War (1870–1) signalled the end of the Second Empire and the imperial couple were sent into exile. Eugénie later lamented, 'at the beginning of the reign I was the *femme futile*, only preoccupied with dresses; and, toward the end of the Empire, I became the *femme fatale* who was held responsible for everything.'[65] A portrait of Eugénie as Marie Antoinette by court artist Franz Xaver Winterhalter captured the silhouette of the crinoline, and the parallels between two consorts whose association with fashion played a part in their demise.

A designer and craftsman, a poet and novelist, a socialist and activist, William Morris was a key voice in the anti-industrialist Arts and Crafts Movement that championed handcrafts and designs inspired by the natural world, as well as folk art and medieval imagery. Morris founded the company Morris, Marshall, Faulkner & Co. in 1861, and the Socialist League 23 years later. Disillusioned with rapid industrialization and believing artisan skills were being lost, he set up the company to design and make by hand wallpaper, textiles, furniture and stained glass, emulating medieval trade guilds. He declared in a lecture in 1880: 'Have nothing in your houses that you do not know to be useful, or believe to be beautiful.' While his anti-machine methods were criticized for producing expensive goods, his artistic and socialist principles were united in his belief that the inequalities of capitalism could be resolved by reinstating handcraft methods and a guild-organized workforce.[66]

William Morris
1834—96

Chemist William Henry Perkin had revolutionized the palette of fashionable dress in 1856, when he created the first artificial dye by accident during an attempt to synthesize quinine to treat malaria. The resulting colour was a brilliant purple that became known as mauve, ensuring purple was no longer the colour of emperors and kings.

Within fifty years there were two thousand chemical dyes.[67] This was one of many areas that Morris railed against, writing in *The Decorator and Furnisher* that this discovery, 'while doing great service to the capitalists in their hunt after profits, has terribly injured the *art* of dyeing, and for the general public has nearly destroyed it as an *art*.'[68] He encouraged a return to vegetable dyes, which produced antique-looking shades that were used in Pre-Raphaelite medieval-inspired artistic dress, as worn by Morris's wife Janey and Dante Gabriel Rossetti's wife Elizabeth Siddall.

The 1960s saw Morris's designs restored to the height of fashion. In 1956 London department store Liberty re-issued original Morris designs, and by the next decade his flowers and foliage were chiming with the revived interest in Art Nouveau and Victoriana.[69] John Pearse, at the boutique Granny Takes a Trip on the King's Road in Chelsea, brought Morris's designs onto the body. He opened the shop with Nigel Waymouth and Sheila Cohen-Pearse in 1966 to sell antique clothing, but began adapting and re-creating the pieces on sale. He used William Morris furnishing fabrics to make tailored garments, one of which subsequently featured on a postage stamp commemorating British design.

Virginia Oldoini was born into Tuscan nobility and married the Count of Castiglione at the age of 17. She was sent to Paris in 1856 on the instruction of her relation Camillo Benso, a key figure in the Italian unification movement, to persuade Emperor Napoleon III of France to support his cause. Paris during the Second Empire was an imperial capital awash with balls and extravagant finery. La Castiglione, as she became known, found fame and notoriety as a great beauty and, briefly, as the Emperor's mistress, leading to the decline of her own marriage. In an age when a woman's looks were her currency, the countess's appearance was compared to classical goddesses and works of art. Journalist and playwright Gaston Jollivet noted that there had never in his lifetime been another woman, 'in whom immortal Venus, as deified by the brushstrokes and chisels of the great masters, was more perfectly incarnate'.[70]

Countess of Castiglione

1837–99

The countess authored and art-directed her own legacy in the photographic studios of Mayer & Pierson, the preferred studio for the glitterati of the Second Empire. The fledgling artform of photography was all the rage, and Pierre-Louis Pierson photographed Castiglione across three periods: her entrance to Paris society in the 1850s, her return in the following decade and a series in the 1890s, towards the end of her life, that served as a morbid coda to the autobiography she documented in clothes.

Castiglione was unique in the number of photographs she had taken of herself and in her level of involvement in creating them. As well as choosing camera angles, she would leave notes for retouchers and even hand-paint images herself, a technique that was very much in vogue. The images ranged from fantastical – dressing as a Breton peasant, a nun, or in the Chinese robes of imperial consorts – to the cataloguing of gowns she had worn to balls, creating a photographic archive of her youth at the court of the Second Empire. Often fashion and fancy dress were intertwined. Keen to highlight her diplomatic stance, she dressed as the ancient Queen of Etruria (a region of central Italy) at a fancy-dress ball in 1863, clad in a tunic-style orange-red velvet dress held together by a brooch, leaving her arms bare. She drew criticism from other guests for the scandalously revealing nature of her costume.[71]

The countess was reclusive for the last years of her life, but many of her pioneering photographs are now held in New York's Metropolitan Museum of Art.

Jules Léotard
c.1838/42–70

French acrobat and aerialist Jules Léotard invented the flying-trapeze circus act, making his debut in 1859 in Paris. A journalist later called him the man 'who defies the law of gravity, who hovers in the air like a bird'.[72] He became known for wearing a *maillot*, a knitted one-piece that did not hinder his performances and showed off his muscular physique, inspiring George Leybourne, of music hall fame, to pen the lyrics:

'A daring young man
on the flying trapeze
His movements were graceful,
all girls he could please.'

This asset did not go unnoticed by Léotard. There is a scandalous account in his memoirs of women testing to see if he padded his *maillot*, and newspapers reported that his ensemble induced women to have provocative dreams about him.[73]

From around 1886, the *maillot* took on the name of its famed wearer. It spread from the circus to ballet studios and informed swimwear designs in the early 20th century, remaining largely as athletic performance wear until the middle of the century when it was first adopted by the fashion world. In 1943's 'The Leotard Idea', *Harper's Bazaar* noted: 'It's a new idea, leading toward the 21st century and the cosmic costumes of Flash Gordon's supergirl...it's an old idea based on every ballet dancer's traditional rehearsal costume.'[74]

The following decade, the leotard took its place in the leisurewear boom of the 1950s, when American designers such as Claire McCardell presented casual sportswear-inspired styles for a postwar population with more disposable income and recreation time, perfect for 'after your swim, for lunch on the beach club terrace or an afternoon of beach sitting'.[75] Leotards and tights became 'campus-fashion fads' that were also attributed to the Beatnik predilection for black tights, as one writer quipped, 'Perhaps the fashion in beatnikkery influenced the craze in beatknittery.' The same writer discussed the rise of 'he-o-tards' for men, the irony of course being that the garment was originally created for male performers.[76]

By the 1960s *Vogue* was celebrating the leotard. Far removed from its sporting origins, it was described as 'a wonderful base for a rush of marvellous looks...Slither it under a sleeveless mink tunic, or a long slit dressing gown of gleaming brocade.'[77]

Empress Myeongseong

1851–95

As the first wife of Gojong of Korea, Empress Myeongseong (as she became known posthumously) was queen consort at a pivotal point in Korean history. Gojong was 26th King of the Chosŏn dynasty, the last Korean dynastic kingdom that ruled for half a millennium until the birth of the Korean Empire in 1897. Myeongseong was brutally assassinated in 1895 under orders of Japan's resident minister in Korea, who believed she was encouraging resistance to Japanese influence. Installed in her place were pro-Japanese politicians, but her murder encouraged widespread anti-Japanese feeling across the nation.[78]

The Chosŏn dynasty was governed by Confucian principles that saw women relegated to the domestic sphere with no formal education. Notions of modesty prohibited engagement in public life.[79] The creation of clothing, from sericulture to weaving and embroidery, was designated as women's work and embedded into the daily lives of women. This was captured in the anonymous poem 'Lament for a Needle': 'When I embroidered phoenixes and peacocks on thick silk or thin, your wondrously agile movements seemed the workings of a spirit'.[80] The phoenix was often used as a decorative motif for the first wife of the king.[81] The Chosŏn period saw the development of the *hanbok*, which came to characterize traditional Korean dress, comprised of skirt (*chima*) and jacket (*jeogori*) for women, and trousers (*baji*) and jacket for men. Translated as 'Korean clothing', the *hanbok* is still worn today for certain festivals and celebrations and in contemporary North Korea can be seen on newsreader Ri Chun-hee.

When the Empress Myeongseong was assassinated, Korea was in the midst of modernizing reforms, which addressed apparel and adornment. The year of her death, under pressure to modernize, King Gojong cut off his *sangtu* (top knot) and issued an edict that other men should follow suit. The *sangtu* was laden with emotional meaning in Korean culture as Confucian philosophy aligned uncut hair with filial piety (respect for one's ancestors). Riots ensued and, according to contemporary sources, horrified peasants murdered some rural officials who followed the ruling.[82] The decree was duly rescinded, but the influence of foreign dress (*yangbok*) had begun. Western clothing was worn in Korea from 1899, when politician Yun Ch'i-o returned from studying abroad wearing a Western suit.[83]

OSCAR WILDE.
Copyright 1882, by N. Sarony.

NEW YORK.

Irish poet and novelist Oscar Wilde was one of the most popular playwrights of the London stage in the early 1890s, and was well known for his *bons mots* that lampooned high society. In 1895 he brought a libel charge against the Marquess of Queensbury, beginning a process that ended with Wilde's incarceration for 'gross indecency'. In the 20th century, Wilde became a heroic symbol of the dawning gay liberation movement.

Oscar Wilde
1854–1900

After arriving in London in the late 1870s, Wilde became as notorious for his dress as for his wit and words. He was a key proponent of the Aesthetic Movement whose philosophy was guided by the principal 'art for art's sake'. The approach applied to all areas of life and was captured in Wilde's aphorism from a lecture in 1884: 'One should either be a work of art or wear a work of art.' This was played out in Wilde's wardrobe through an interest in historical styles, such as knee breeches and stockings, and affected accessories from sunflowers to green carnations. Wilde later turned to a simpler mode of dress and embraced dandyism.[84]

The department store Liberty, founded in 1875, became a crucial destination for the Aesthetic shopper. The association of Liberty with the movement was so clear that when the Gilbert & Sullivan comic opera *Patience* premiered in 1881, satirizing the Aesthetic Movement, including Wilde, the costumes were made from Liberty fabrics, and the store even advertised in the programme.[85] Aesthetic dress was characterized by a return to pre-industrial dyes and techniques, and a rejection of the tight-laced corset. In this respect, it shared ideas with other dress-reform movements in the UK, such as the Rational Dress Society, which was supported by Wilde's wife Constance.

From 1887 to 1889, Wilde edited a women's periodical. Under his editorship he transformed *The Lady's World: A Magazine of Fashion and Society* into the intellectually driven and artistic title *The Woman's World*, for which Constance also wrote. Wilde made his feelings about mainstream fashion clear in an article penned for the *New York Tribune* in 1885, titled 'The Philosophy of Dress': 'Fashion is ephemeral. Art is eternal. Indeed what is a fashion really? A fashion is merely a form of ugliness so absolutely unbearable that we have to alter it every six months!' Wilde used dress to express his bohemianism and pursuit of beauty, in opposition to what he saw as bourgeois Victorian values.

In 1892 Keir Hardie was elected as Member of Parliament (MP) for West Ham South in London, and the following year was a founder member of the Independent Labour Party. Coming from the slums of Glasgow, Hardie had worked since the age of seven, first as a delivery boy and then in the coal mines of Ayrshire. Having no formal education, he learned to read and write as an adult, later writing for the *Ardrossan & Saltcoats Herald* and editing *The Labour Leader*. His experience of working life, trade unions and the inequities of British society led to his staunch belief in socialism.

Keir Hardie
1856–1915

Hardie was not the first working-class MP in Westminster, but he was the first to highlight his class origins through his choice of dress. Newspaper accounts varied in their descriptions, but it is likely that on his entry to Parliament Hardie wore a tweed suit and a deerstalker cap, which became his trademark. This was smart working-class dress, rather than labouring clothing, but against the MP's uniform look of frock coat and silk top hat, it caused an uproar. The *Telegraph* commented: 'The House is neither a coal store, a smithy nor a carpenter's shop; and, therefore, the entrance of Mr Keir Hardie in a blue serge coat and vest, yellow checked trousers, and a flannel shirt which carried no collar upon it, left a painful impression which the workman's tweed cap was powerless to subdue.'[86] The *Birmingham Daily Post* suggested that his 'symbolic apparel' had been selected 'for the sake of cheap and tawdry notoriety', while *Reynolds's Newspaper* remarked, 'The House of Commons – the representatives of the people – are scandalized'.[87] Claiming the decision was not deliberate, Hardie stated: 'I have always worn a tweed cap and homespun clothes and it never entered my head to make a change.'[88] However, in 1887, he had written that if a local man were elected, 'he should go to the House of Commons in workaday clothes'.[89]

Friedrich Engels, co-author of *The Communist Manifesto*, wrote about clothing as a marker of class identity in 1845. He noted that fustian, a coarse cloth of cotton and linen, 'has become the proverbial costume of the working men, who are called "fustian jackets", and call themselves so in contrast to the gentlemen who wear broadcloth'.[90] Hardie's working-class dress was arguably a factor in the growing popular support for the labour movement throughout the UK.

Annie Oakley

1860–1926

Born Phoebe Ann Moses, Mosey or Mozee to a Quaker family in Ohio, Annie Oakley became a sharpshooting star, touring the USA and Europe displaying her firearm skills. From 1885 she toured with Buffalo Bill's Wild West Show, performing shooting tricks with mirrors and on horseback. Throughout her career, Annie designed and made her own costumes, which featured lavish embroidery and fringing.[91] Due to her Quaker background her costumes were never too revealing or risqué, and she disliked wearing make-up.[92] Often derided for her occupation in the 'masculine' realm of shooting, Oakley was keen to maintain a traditionally feminine appearance for her late-19th-century audiences.

The costumes that Oakley made and wore included exaggerated elements of frontier dress. Like much original 'Western' clothing, the decorative fringing and embroidery were influenced by Native American embellishment, and leather or buckskin was used for practicality, being more hard-wearing than wool. Buffalo Bill, born William Frederick Cody (1846–1917), was a frontier scout and hunter before he moved into show business. In 1871 General Henry Eugene Davies described Cody in his frontier garb: 'Dressed in a suit of light buckskin, trimmed along the seams with fringes of the same leather, his costume lighted by the crimson shirt worn under his open coat, a broad sombrero on his head, and carrying his rifle lightly in his hand...he realized to perfection the bold hunter and gallant sportsman of the plains.'[93] This had become the recognized look of the prairie scout. Cody toured his successful show between 1883 and 1916, which played a key part in the early global mythologizing of the American West, and in the transition of cowboy clothing from workwear to fashionable dress.[94]

In the 1940s and 1950s Annie Oakley was immortalized on stage and screen in the Rodgers and Hammerstein production, *Annie Get Your Gun*. It ran on Broadway and was turned into a film in 1950, and a television series, *Annie Oakley*, screened in the mid-1950s. These translated into fashions for women and young girls. In 1946 Russeks department store sold rayon prints featuring a 'panoramic frontier setting' with motifs including 'sharp-shooting targets' to tie in with the Broadway show.[95] A television promotion for girls included three-piece outfits with leather fringing and dresses 'with a target and rifle trademark embroidered on slash pockets'. These could be worn with beaded moccasin slippers or elk-leather boots.[96] Elements of Western frontier dress had become marketable symbols of the American dream.

Cross-dressing has historically been more acceptable within the subversive space of the theatre, from Shakespeare to the 'breeches roles' of the Restoration that found favour with the first actresses such as Nell Gwyn. Vesta Tilley (born Matilda Alice Powles) made her fortune as a male impersonator in the music halls of the 19th century. With the help of her father (who

Vesta Tilley
1864–1952

worked the halls) she first trod the boards at the age of three and a half. At six she performed her first routine in male clothing. She believed there was more scope with male roles, and, in her own words, 'female costume was rather a drag.'[97]

Vesta Tilley was such a successful male impersonator that she even made the men's fashion pages. The 'As Seen by Him' column in American *Vogue* stated in 1894, 'anyone who wishes to see a very well-fitting morning costume, frock coat and dittoes [sic], should go to hear Vesta Tilley...Her waistcoat is bad and her tie preposterous, but the rest of the costume admirable. It fits well, and everything is in keeping.'[98] The following year the

same feature consisted of a fashion spread illustrated by Vesta in an 'extreme English frock coat', evening dress and naval dress, among others.[99] She also claimed in her memoirs to have licensed a range of 'Vesta Tilley Boaters' with a firm of outfitters, along with Vesta Tilley waistcoats, cigars and cufflinks.[100]

Tilley toured the music halls in the UK and the USA, and her popularity reached an all-time high during World War I when she ran a recruitment drive that earned her the nickname 'Britain's best recruiting sergeant'. After the war, her husband, music hall impresario and later MP, Walter de Frece, was knighted, so Vesta essentially became part of the upper echelons of society that she often parodied in her performances. Despite stints as a sailor and a soldier, Vesta Tilley really left her mark as a rakish man-about-town, paving the way for successive generations of female performers to don formal male attire. Women in suits have become some of our most enduring fashion icons, from Marlene Dietrich (who, in her autobiography, partly credited Vesta Tilley for her white-tie look) to Catherine Deneuve wearing Yves Saint Laurent's 'Le Smoking' and, more recently, Janelle Monáe.

Sadayakko Kawakami
1871–1946

Also known as Sada Yacco, Sadayakko trained as a geisha of the first rank, but left the profession to marry and become an actress alongside her husband Otojirō Kawakami of the Japanese Court Company. Labelled *soshi shibai* (or even 'new theatre'), Kawakami's subversive style mixed traditional Kabuki elements with Western conventions, and the company was the first legitimate Japanese theatre group to perform in the West. Sada Yacco was breaking new ground by appearing with an all-male troupe. From 1899 they embarked on an international tour. Labelled 'Japan's Ellen Terry' in the USA, Sadayakko made the cover of *Harper's Bazaar* in March 1900. *Vogue* praised her costumes as 'exquisite in design, weave, and texture',[101] and she received rave reviews in London and at the Paris Exposition Universelle of 1900.[102]

In 1853 US forces had coerced Japan to open its ports to international trade, ending centuries of isolation. The Meiji Restoration in 1868 consolidated power under the rule of Emperor Meiji, who began to actively promote trade and modernization. A crucial element of this was dress reform, and the emperor and empress encouraged Western clothes for public life.[103] It was from contact with Western dress that the word 'kimono' evolved. Literally translated as 'thing to wear', it came to replace *kosode*, which referred to a particular type of garment that had developed over centuries. The diverse robes worn in Japan were now defined in relation to Western clothing, and the kimono became the national dress of Japan.[104]

1900   OCTOBRE – II   N° 44

LE THÉATRE

DIRECTION ET RÉDACTION :
24, Boulevard des Capucines.

PUBLICITÉ :
DUHAMEL et COMMUNAY, seuls concessionnaires
19, Boulevard Montmartre.

CONDITIONS DE L'ABONNEMENT :
PARIS : 1 an . . . 40 fr. | DÉPARTEMENTS : 1 an 44 fr.
ÉTRANGER (Union postale) : 1 an . . 52 fr.

ABONNEMENT ET VENTE :
Librairie du FIGARO, 26, rue Drouot.

Cliché P. Nadar.

THÉATRE LOIE FULLER (Rue de Paris). — Mme SADA YACCO. — Rôle de la Ghésha. — *LA GHESHA ET LE CHEVALIER*

ÉDITEURS : *Manzi, Joyant & Cie*, *24, Boulevard des Capucines, Paris.* — PRIX NET : **2 fr.** ; Étranger, **2 fr. 50**

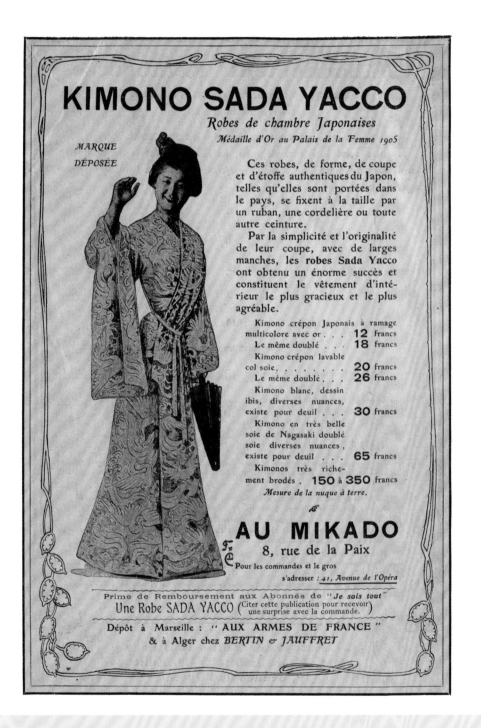

KIMONO SADA YACCO

Robes de chambre Japonaises

Médaille d'Or au Palais de la Femme 1905

MARQUE
DÉPOSÉE

Ces robes, de forme, de coupe et d'étoffe authentiques du Japon, telles qu'elles sont portées dans le pays, se fixent à la taille par un ruban, une cordelière ou toute autre ceinture.

Par la simplicité et l'originalité de leur coupe, avec de larges manches, les **robes Sada Yacco** ont obtenu un énorme succès et constituent le vêtement d'intérieur le plus gracieux et le plus agréable.

Kimono crépon Japonais à ramage multicolore avec or . . . **12** francs
Le même doublé . . . **18** francs
Kimono crépon lavable col soie. . . **20** francs
Le même doublé . . . **26** francs
Kimono blanc, dessin ibis, diverses nuances, existe pour deuil . . . **30** francs
Kimono en très belle soie de Nagasaki doublé soie diverses nuances, existe pour deuil . . . **65** francs
Kimonos très richement brodés . **150** à **350** francs
Mesure de la nuque à terre.

AU MIKADO

8, rue de la Paix

Pour les commandes et le gros

s'adresser : *41, Avenue de l'Opéra*

Prime de Remboursement aux Abonnés de "*Je sais tout*"
Une Robe SADA YACCO (Citer cette publication pour recevoir une surprise avec la commande.)

Dépôt à Marseille : "AUX ARMES DE FRANCE"
& à Alger chez *BERTIN & JAUFFRET*

By the late 1890s, European and Japanese dress was entwined in a circular relationship of influence. Japanese art had been revered by European collectors since the middle of the 19th century and was impacting the Belle Époque designs of Art Nouveau. One London review described Sada Yacco 'as if she had walked out of an Outamaro or Hiroshige print'.[105] Stores such as Takashimaya expanded into international markets with 'shops for foreigners' across Japan and in Lyon and London, creating specific products for the Western market.[106]

As debates raged in Japan about dress, modernity and national identity, Sada Yacco fuelled the vogue for Japanese styles in Europe. She had form as a trendsetter: since the 18th century, geishas had been fashion leaders, from their choice of colours to the folds of their obi, and they had been among the first women to adopt Western clothing.[107] The boutique Au Mikado in Paris offered dressing gowns inspired by the actress, often modelled with the Edwardian corseted silhouette, and the kimono has been reimagined endlessly in Western dress.

It was from contact with Western dress that the word 'kimono' evolved. Literally translated as 'thing to wear'.

Known by her stage name La Macarrona, Juana Vargas de las Heras was a flamenco *bailaora* (dancer) during the golden age of the artform. Also referred to as 'Queen of the Gypsies', La Macarrona hailed from a Gitano (Spanish Romany) family in Andalusia and counted a number of other flamenco artists among her relatives. She danced in Spain's *café cantantes* (café concerts), which emerged in the middle of the 19th century as café society was flourishing throughout Europe, and first performed internationally at the Paris World's Fair in 1889.

Juana La Macarrona
1860/70–1947

Flamenco is the product of cross-cultural contact in Andalusia,[108] predominantly Gitano and Andalusian culture and musical traditions. As such, flamenco grew in popularity from the late 18th century, when King Charles III of Spain relaxed laws that persecuted Romany Gypsies (who had arrived in Andalusia from the 15th century).[109] It became known as flamenco the following century, when it moved out of the family home and into public spaces.

The flamenco dancer's costume is centred on the *bata de cola* – a flounced dress with a train which fully developed in the 1890s – which is thought to be based on Gitana clothing.[110] Previous laws that demanded assimilation or exile of the Spanish Romany population often forbade the wearing of distinctive clothing associated with Gypsies.[111] Yet throughout the 1800s, as the flounced skirt and shawl became the recognizable Gitana ensemble, these styles regularly found their way into the wardrobes of fashionable Spanish women. Just four years after La Macarrona danced at the Paris World's Fair, a writer claimed: 'the bright gala-dress of the gitana has become fashionable among high-placed señoras who appear at dance or salon sporting the gaudy Manila shawl with its flowing fringe, short frock, and with hair coiffured *a la Flamenca*.'[112]

The Manila shawl is a heavily embroidered, fringed shawl that originated in China, but by the 1920s it was internationally associated with Spanish dress and identity.[113] By the early 20th century polka dots were one of the most popular prints for flamenco dresses, and stripes, florals and bright plaids also appeared.[114] As Juana La Macarrona was popularizing flamenco, the costume became the symbol for Andalusia and an emblem of Spanish national identity itself. This subsequently inspired Spanish designers such as Cristóbal Balenciaga, who often featured the flamenco flounce in his evening dresses.

Born Marie of Edinburgh, granddaughter of Queen Victoria, Marie married Crown Prince Ferdinand in 1893, and went on to become the last Queen Consort of Romania in 1914. She often wore local dress to increase her popularity in her new country, and particularly took to folk motifs such as embroidery. This gave her a distinctive look compared to other European leaders of the day, such as Alexandra of Denmark, wife of King Edward VII of England. Alexandra was known for setting trends of a very different kind, much more in line with conventional corseted late 19th- and early 20th-century fashions.[115]

Queen Marie of Romania

1875–1938

It has been suggested that Marie explicitly adopted folk styles while she was Crown Princess in the aftermath of the Romanian Peasants' Revolt of 1907, which was violently crushed by the authorities. By 1909 she was being photographed in prestigious fashion magazines, posing with her children in the forest of Sinaia 'in the picturesque garb of the peasants'.[116] Marie's mother was descended from the Romanov Tsars in Russia, where a folk and peasant revival had flourished throughout the late 19th century,[117] and Marie's predilection for traditional folk styles started fashion trends among young upper-class women.

ROYAL "PEASANTS" IN THE FOREST OF SINAIA

IT IS A PRETTY CUSTOM OF THE CROWN PRINCESS OF ROUMANIA TO DRESS HERSELF AND HER CHILDREN IN THE PICTURESQUE GARB OF THE PEASANTS WHEN AT THEIR SUMMER PALACE

Throughout the 1920s, embroidery from Romania, Hungary and Russia was a popular feature of the London and Paris collections.[118] Coco Chanel employed the Russian folk-embroidery house, Kitmar, to adorn many of her pieces, and the company's founder, Maria Pavlovna, even created some of the needlework designs.[119] Queen Marie began to be celebrated as a fashion icon at the same time as peasant dress and life were romanticized, as increased urbanization and mass-manufacture were thought to be putting traditional handcrafts at risk. The romanticization of peasant life was often explored through clothing. A report in American *Vogue* from the wedding of Queen Marie's daughter in 1922 noted the 'embroidered costumes of the peasants gleamed like great butterflies'.[120]

Outside of Romania, Marie was known for her patronage of companies and couture houses that specialized in embroidery, such as Chéruit in Paris and Liberty in London.[121] Her fashion sense was lauded abroad: Lady Susan Townley praised her 'truly regal taste in dress' in the British magazine *Arts & Decoration*,[122] and American *Vogue* noted that Marie was 'famed for beauty, wit and taste' and included her recommendations for pieces from design houses Lelong and Patou.[123] A later article included sketches of Romanian peasant clothing and praised local embroidery as 'delicate stitchery of exquisite design and colouring', while Queen Marie was commended for having 'energetically fostered the cause of national art'.[124]

20th & 21st Centuries

Italian heiress Marchesa Casati declared, 'I want to be a living work of art', and dedicated her life to this pursuit. Luisa's parents died when she was a teenager, leaving her incredibly wealthy at a young age. She married Camillo, Marchese Casati Stampa di Soncino in 1900, but they lived separately for much of their marriage, and she conducted a public affair with writer and poet Gabriele D'Annunzio, who wrote, 'she was akin to the greatest creatures of Michelangelo'.[1] She had a striking appearance, powdering her face a ghoulish white, turning her hair red with henna and excessively ringing her eyes with black kohl. Casati provided a blueprint for bohemianism and fashioned herself into the ultimate muse. Among many others, she was photographed by Man Ray and Baron de Meyer, painted by Augustus John and Giovanni Boldini, and had her head sculpted by Jacob Epstein and Giacomo Balla.

In 1910 Casati took over the ruins of Palazzo Venier dei Leoni on the Grand Canal in Venice, which she used as a setting for a number of elaborate costume parties. Her dress outside of masquerade was no less dramatic, as photographer Baron de Meyer wrote in *Vogue* in 1916: 'The Marchesa Casati, at sunset, reclining in her gondola, wrapped in tiger skins and fondling her favourite leopard, is a sight to be seen only in Venice.'[2] Her other pets included parrots, monkeys, peacocks and snakes that would travel with her in satin-lined boxes ordered from jewelers.[3]

At odds with the beauty ideals of the era, Casati ushered in avant-garde modernism in dress, patronizing couturiers such as Poiret, known for his Orientalist designs, and Fortuny, known for reviving historic techniques and experimenting with dyes. Her theatrical style was aided by Léon Bakst, costume designer for the Ballets Russes, whom she commissioned to create clothing for both costume balls and daily life.

In her later years in Paris, she was known to attach gilded ram's horns to her temples and could be seen stalking the streets in a black velvet dress, black eye patch and tiger-skin top hat, accompanied by a miniature crocodile on a lead.[4] Marchesa Casati's legacy lives on through the art she inspired and the design houses she continues to influence, including Dries Van Noten, Karl Lagerfeld, John Galliano, Alexander McQueen and Tom Ford.

Luisa, Marchesa Casati Stampa di Soncino

1881—1957

A key figure in the British suffragette movement, Christabel Pankhurst, and her mother Emmeline, founded the militant Women's Social and Political Union (WSPU) in October 1903, with the slogan 'Deeds, not words'. Opponents to the suffrage cause often 'masculinized' suffragettes, depicting them as unnatural with short hair, ties and collars.[5] Dressing fashionably was an ideological issue, as the WSPU's newspaper, *Votes for Women*, noted in 1908: 'Dress…is at all times a matter of importance, whether she [the suffragette] is to appear on a public platform, a procession, or merely in house or street about her ordinary vocations.'[6]

shades in autumn and winter fashions. Almost every shop window is showing purple hats and green hats, purple ties and green ties, purple cloth gowns and green cloth gowns in endless variety.'[8]

Votes for Women embedded fashion into its coverage from 1908. The rise of the department store in the mid-19th century had seen a gradual shift in the lives of middle-class women, offering a safe public space and a gradual element of emancipation. Stores such as Marshall & Snelgrove, Swan & Edgar, Peter Robinson, Whiteleys, Debenham & Freebody, Harrods and especially Selfridges all became advertisers in the suffrage press.

Dame Christabel Pankhurst
1880—1958

While in exile in Paris, Christabel edited the WSPU's second newspaper, *Suffragette*, from its inauguration in 1912. So great was the consumer power of middle-class suffragettes that when the paper advocated window smashing and arson in West End stores, targeted companies continued to advertise in the paper.[9]

WSPU member Emmeline Pethick-Lawrence devised the group's colour scheme of white, green and purple, with the aim of politicizing appearance so suffragettes could easily be spotted in the street.[7] *Votes for Women*, which was edited by Pethick-Lawrence, observed the impact these colours were having on wider fashions, reporting: 'One cannot walk down Bond Street and the neighbourhood without being struck by the fact that our colours are evidently going to be the leading

Activism halted during World War I, and in 1918 the Representation of the People Act gave the vote to women aged thirty and over, with certain caveats. In 1928 the Equal Franchise Act was passed, giving equal voting rights to men.

Mati Hari

1876–1917

Exotic dancer turned double agent, Mata Hari is one of the most enduring myths of the 20th century and the archetypal *femme fatale* spy. Born Margaretha Zelle in the Netherlands, the woman who became known to the world as Mata Hari married a Dutch colonial army officer and spent time in the Dutch East Indies, mainly Sumatra and Java, which provided inspiration for her later 'Eastern' performances. The marriage was abusive and the couple separated after returning to Europe, where Margaretha Zelle reinvented herself as the dancer and courtesan Mata Hari.[10]

Mata Hari's performances caused a sensation in the salons of early 20th-century Paris.[11] Her costumes, created by Erté, among others, played a key role in this. *Vogue* enthused: 'Her costume is composed of chains of jewels in massive gold and silver settings, and elaborately carved breastplates; and on her head are gorgeous ornaments...The skirts are made entirely of veils in brilliant reds, greens, and yellows...they fall in soft folds and envelope her body, like the blossoming petals of a flower.'[12]

Despite the release of declassified records in 2017, it is still unclear whether Mata Hari was a double agent. The majority of accounts suggest that she was not, yet she was executed by firing squad in 1917, becoming a legend. The case rested on very little evidence, and in 1930 the German government exculpated her. She has become a symbol of the scapegoating of 'unruly' women and the fear of uncontained female sexuality.

The myth of Mata Hari as seductive temptress has persisted in popular culture. The 1931 film, *Mata Hari*, starred Greta Garbo and was directed by George Fitzmaurice and costumed by Adrian. The costumes were sent on a tour of the USA and became bestsellers when available for retail.[13] *Vogue* discussed the long coat with wide sable lapels and tiny pillbox hats that were worn in the film, stating: 'All these and more Garbo fashions have had a tremendous influence on women's clothes.'[14] Another film, *Mata Hari, Agent H21* (Jean-Louis Richard, 1964), starred Jeanne Moreau and was costumed by Pierre Cardin, whose sketches were printed in *Women's Wear Daily*. Cardin was praised for bringing back a period that was 'bound to inspire Paris', recalling 'the splendor of 1908 through 1915 fashions.'[15]

A champion swimmer, vaudeville performer and silent-movie star, Annette Kellerman had a significant impact on attitudes towards swimwear and modesty in the early 20th century. As *Harper's Bazaar* noted in 1916, she was 'A star who has put swimming and other aquatic sports on the movie map.'[16]

Annette Kellerman
1886/7–1975

Born in Sydney, Kellerman took up swimming to overcome childhood rickets. By 1902 she was winning titles and began performing a mermaid act, swimming with fish at the Melbourne Exhibition Aquarium.[17] She was soon touring the world, amazing crowds by swimming the Thames, attempting to swim the English Channel and performing in a glass tank at the New York Hippodrome (for which she has been called the grandmother of synchronized swimming).[18]

Kellerman railed against the prevailing restrictions in swimwear, lambasting the impractical nature of the bathing dress and bloomers of the era. This culminated in her arrest in 1907 on a beach in Massachusetts on a charge of indecent exposure, as her skintight one-piece swimsuit was deemed far too revealing. While this is likely to have been a publicity stunt, the ensuing popularity of the design ensured that she is often credited with being the 'originator of the one-piece bathing suit', which became known colloquially as

She is often credited as the
'originator of the one–piece
bathing suit.'

an 'Annette Kellerman'.[19] Furthermore, she was judged by a Harvard doctor to be the 'perfect woman' as her proportions most closely mirrored those of the Ancient Greek statue *Venus de Milo*. She used this as a selling point for her health regimes and fitness books, which she advertised regularly in American *Vogue* and *Harper's Bazaar*.

Kellerman was snapped up by the movie industry for films from *The Mermaid* (1911) to *Venus of the South Seas* (1924).[20] She used flesh-coloured tights to give the illusion of nudity, but stills from films such as *A Daughter of the Gods* (1916) show her naked, granting her the title of first major film star to appear in a nude scene. A reviewer remarked at the time: 'Clothes may make the man but they don't make a daughter of the gods, at least not the sort Annette depicts.'[21]

Kellerman was immortalized in *Million Dollar Mermaid* (1952), choreographed by Busby Berkeley, in which she was played by swimming star Esther Williams. Kellerman returned to live in Australia before she died, and her costume collection can be found at the Powerhouse Museum in Sydney.

A ballet dancer from a young age, Vaslav Nijinsky joined the Ballets Russes in 1909, the year the company was founded by impresario Sergei Diaghilev, who became Nijinsky's lover. The troupe was a *gesamtkunstwerk* of Modernist art and design, working with musicians, artists and fashion designers, from Igor Stravinsky and Claude Debussy to Pablo Picasso and Coco Chanel. Nijinsky was ousted from the Ballets Russes after he angered Diaghilev by marrying Romola de Pulszky in 1913. He was diagnosed with schizophrenia in 1919 and spent much of his life institutionalized.

The Ballets Russes premiered in Paris in 1909 and quickly became a sensation, as noted three years later in American *Vogue*: 'The Ballet Russe [sic] has grown to be a feature of the theatre season in Paris... A storm of criticism greeted the first performance of *L'Après-midi d'un Faune*, but when I saw it the audience was wildly enthusiastic. Nijinsky is really wonderful.'[22] *L'Après-midi d'un Faune* (*The Afternoon of a Faun*), choreographed by Nijinsky, had been criticized for its overtly erotic nature. Nijinsky was renowned for his remarkable leaps, and could dance *en pointe*, which was unusual for a male dancer.

Vaslav Nijinsky
1889–1950

In 1913 more scandal ensued with the debut of *Le Sacre du printemps* (*The Rite of Spring*) at the Théâtre des Champs-Elysées. Choreographed by Nijinsky and costumed by Nicholas Roerich, the piece was based on Russian folklore, folk dress and folk music. The composition and performance was so antithetical to classical ballet that some reports claimed there were riots at the opening night.

There was a synergy between the Ballets Russes and Paris fashion.[23] Orientalist creations by costume designer Léon Bakst for ballets such as *Schéhérazade* were often compared to the designs of Paul Poiret, who was also inspired by theatrical Eastern themes. Bakst also collaborated with the couturier Jeanne Paquin, as well as dressing society women with a flair for flamboyance. He is said to have claimed: 'I was born...in order to revive among my contemporaries the beautiful and fresh colour misunderstood and stifled for so long a time by people of taste.'[24]

Nijinsky also set fashions. The ballet *Le Pavillon d'Armide* premiered in St Petersburg, then opened in Paris in 1909. According to Nijinsky's wife, his particular way of wearing his choker tight around his neck was copied: 'Cartier quickly took note of this novel idea, and socially ladies in Paris and London were soon wearing close-fitting chokers of black moiré silk, diamonds, and pearls *à l'Armide*.'[25]

Ballets Russes productions continue to be performed today, and its impact on fashion is extensive, from Yves Saint Laurent's winter 1976 'Russian' collection, to Erdem Moralioglu, who even researched the company's archives at the V&A.[26]

Oskar Schlemmer first joined the influential Bauhaus art school in 1921 as head of the sculpture workshop, and he went on to run the theatre workshop from 1923. The Bauhaus was founded by Modernist architect Walter Gropius in Weimar, Germany, in 1919, and fused crafts with fine art through a number of workshops ranging from metalwork to textiles. The theatre workshop, run by Schlemmer with abstract painter and stage designer László Moholy-Nagy, combined architecture, painting, sculpture, music and dance.

Oskar Schlemmer
1888–1943

Schlemmer's key interest was the abstraction of the human form, as he explained: 'The transformation of the human body, its metamorphosis, is made possible by the *costume*, the disguise.'[27] This led to a fascination with masks, which reached an apex with his use of puppets and marionettes, and was brought to life in his most famous production, *The Triadic Ballet*, the first entire performance of which was staged in 1922 at Stuttgart Landestheater.[28]

The monumental parties thrown at the Bauhaus put costume and sets to good effect. Parties and festivals were integral to life and learning at the Bauhaus and were often fronted by the theatre workshop, which would create the decor and clothing. Themes ranged from the Beard, Nose and Heart Party to the White Party, in which revellers were asked to dress in two-thirds white, one-third spotted, checked or striped. The Metal Party took things even further: costumes consisted of tin foil, frying pans and spoons, and the event was entered by sliding down a chute into a room filled with the sound of bells and decorated with silver balls.

The Nazis closed the Bauhaus school in 1933 because they believed it was aligned with Bolshevism and a breeding ground for so-called 'degenerate art'. However, the Bauhaus has an extensive legacy in every design medium. As Walter Gropius remarked: 'My own great impression of Schlemmer's stage work was to see and experience his magic of transforming dancers and actors into moving architecture.'[29] This approach can still be felt in both costume design and fashion, and was brought to life in the editorial 'Human Building Blocks' in *Dazed & Confused* magazine in October 2008, which also paid homage to the 1931 Beaux-Arts Ball that saw architects dress as their own buildings.

In 1949 American *Vogue* declared: 'In every age there is one man in public life who dresses with outstanding grace and distinction...Certainly in our time it is H.R.H. the Duke of Windsor.'[30] The Duke of Windsor was a title created for King Edward VIII, who reigned for nearly 11 months, abdicating in 1936 to marry Wallis Simpson, a woman who was not only American, but was also married to someone else at the time they met. Their wedding the following year at the Château de Candé in the Loire Valley was covered by Cecil Beaton in American *Vogue*, and showed Wallis Simpson in a grey-blue wedding dress by Mainbocher.[31] The couple lived in exile for the rest of their lives.

Duke Of Windsor
1894–1972

The Duke also broke with convention in his wardrobe. As the Prince of Wales, his casual, modern and etiquette-snubbing panache set countless trends in menswear and womenswear that were covered in the fashion and trade press, from Fair Isle sweaters to plus fours, berets, yellow golfing and hunting shirts, Aertex shirts and patterned golf stockings. American *Vogue* even credited him with the revival of scarf-making in northern English and Scottish mills.[32] He had his suit jackets cut by Frederick Scholte of Savile Row and his trousers cut in New York, as he preferred a wider, more casual style. It was this combination that formed his distinctive look in contrasting checks and plaids. His consistent breaks with tradition were often the source of tension between him and his father, George V, but he was not a complete iconoclast as he continued to dress for dinner, even when at home, throughout his life.[33]

In the 1960s the Duke's style garnered a new following, and American *Vogue* noted: 'Unique and zesty, the Duke of Windsor... has through his incomparable elegance and grace influenced a whole generation born years after he left the throne of Great Britain.'[34] It is clear that the Duke cut a dash throughout his life, and his sartorial prowess was influential on both sides of the Atlantic. However, it is crucial not to romanticize his legacy: he is widely believed to have been a Nazi sympathizer, and Edward and Wallis took an unofficial trip to Germany in 1937, which culminated in a meeting with the Führer. Had Germany been victorious in World War II, Hitler planned to reinstate Edward as king with Wallis as his queen.[35]

Abstract artist Sonia Delaunay was a key figure of the Parisian avant-garde. She worked across disciplines and claimed: 'For me, there was no gap between my painting and what is called my "decorative" work...I never considered the "minor arts" to be artistically frustrating; on the contrary, it was an extension of my art, it showed me new ways, while using the same method.'[36] Born in Ukraine, raised in St Petersburg and educated in Germany, Delaunay lived in Paris for much of her life. In 1964 she became the first living female artist to have a retrospective exhibition at the Louvre.

Sonia Delaunay

1885–1979

In 1910 Sonia married the artist Robert Delaunay. His study of colour led to his theory of Simultaneism, which combined contrasting colours to express movement in painting. Sonia created her first *robe simultanée* (simultaneous dress) in 1913 by sewing patches of fabric together. The garment experimented with colour and shape and would come to embody Delaunay's hallmark style, fusing Russian folk art with Parisian avant-garde, and the artisanal with the modern. Robert later noted that she 'created her harmonies and rhythms of color from life itself...In short, the surface of the fabric, intimate

with the surroundings of everyday life, presents something like visual movements comparable to chords in music.'[37]

Commercial opportunities became a priority after Delaunay's family property was seized in the Russian Revolution. She had been living in Spain and set up the successful Casa Sonia to sell interior decoration and Simultaneous clothing. In 1921 Sonia, Robert and their son returned to Paris and Delaunay began experimenting with *robes poèmes*, embroidering friends' poems onto textiles and clothes. In 1925 she founded Maison Delaunay and ran *la Boutique Simultanée* at the International Exhibition of Modern Decorative and Industrial Arts in Paris, displaying a range of coats, bags, shoes and scarves created by Russian seamstresses and embroiderers. Film star Gloria Swanson and heiress and activist Nancy Cunard were customers.

The maison folded in the wake of the Wall Street Crash of 1929, but the vision lived on through her textile company, Tissus Delaunay. She also had a long-running relationship with Metz & Co department store in Amsterdam, which produced and sold her designs into the 1960s.[38] Throughout her illustrious career, Delaunay successfully marketed her avant-garde abstract designs without compromising her ethos of colour, movement and rhythm.

A tennis superstar and trailblazer, Suzanne Lenglen was one of the earliest celebrity players. *Harper's Bazaar* noted, when she was just 17, that whenever she played 'there is always sure to be a throng'.[39] She won the Wimbledon singles title six times, as well as many other prestigious championships throughout her career. When she started out, it had not been long since women played in bustles and petticoats, and the Wimbledon women's dressing room still had a bar for hanging sweat-soaked (and often blood-stained) corsets to dry.[40]

costumes are correct and chic on the court and after the game'[42]) and claims in *Harper's Bazaar* that she 'revolutionised dressing on the courts'.[43] Patou was an innovator in the realm of high-fashion sportswear, and Lenglen became a director of the sports department at his couture house.[44] Their collaboration came at a time when sport and outdoor pursuits were becoming more acceptable for women, and fashionable. Lenglen also promoted a range of tennis dresses with department store Selfridges, which advertised in *Tatler*.[45]

Suzanne Lenglen
1899–1938

Lenglen favoured designs by couturier Jean Patou, whose dresses were sleeveless with short hemlines. Clad in his designs and her signature bandeau, Lenglen was praised not only for being stylish, but also for wearing clothing appropriate for her sport: *à la mode* but also thoroughly modern. As noted by American *Vogue* in 1926: 'Mademoiselle Lenglen, the French champion, wears a tennis costume that is extraordinarily chic in the freedom, the suitability, and the excellence of its simple lines.'[41]

Her affiliation with Patou led to fashion spreads in *Vogue* ('Her Jean Patou sports

Lenglen turned professional in 1926, no easy feat in a world that still expected its players to come from wealthy enough backgrounds to maintain their amateur status. Playing for money was believed to be gauche, an opinion that prompted Fred Perry (the son of a cotton spinner turned Labour MP) to call Wimbledon 'the most snobbish centre of sport in the world'.[46] During the interwar era, a number of tennis stars, notably René Lacoste and Fred Perry, drew on their burgeoning celebrity along with their understanding of functional yet smart sportswear to create items and brands that are still around today. The journey from court to atelier continues with the success of lines such as EleVen by Venus Williams.

Poet and author Radclyffe Hall wrote the groundbreaking lesbian novel *The Well of Loneliness*, which cemented her status as an icon of lesbian, queer and, at times, transgender identities.[47] In 1928 the novel was banned in a trial that labelled it 'an obscene libel' and 'an offence to public decency'.[48] Focusing on protagonist Stephen Gordon, the book has been described as, 'a manifesto for a certain kind of lesbian "mannishness"',[49] and Gordon's interest in dress is evident throughout the work. The attention to detail is comparable to Beau Brummell's dandyism (*see* page 126):

Radclyffe Hall
1880–1943

'She ordered not one new suit but three, and she also ordered a pair of brown shoes; indeed she spent most of the afternoon in ordering things for her personal adornment. She heard herself being ridiculously fussy about details, disputing with her tailor over buttons…disputing regarding the match of her ties with the young man who sold her handkerchiefs and neckties – for such trifles had assumed an enormous importance.'

Hall, who lived with Una Vincenzo (Lady Troubridge) for many years, was known for wearing masculine styles herself. A local newspaper report in 1928 noted, 'she may frequently be seen at West End theatres dressed in what is, save for a tight skirt, a gentleman's evening suit, with white waistcoat complete. She wears her Titian hair in a close Eton crop.'[50]

Literature circulated among educated groups that focused on a notion of 'sexual inversion' as outlined by sexologists such as Richard von Krafft-Ebbing and Havelock Ellis, who medicalized homosexuality. Outdated by 21st-century standards, Ellis wrote in 1895 that 'sexually inverted' women had a 'pronounced tendency to adopt male attire'.[51]

'Mannishness', however, was a term that also gained currency in contemporary fashion parlance, as a more mature version of the *garçonne* look that was all the rage in London and Paris. This is evident in a 1926 Harrods advert that publicized skirt suits, 'with a hint of mannish severity in their trim lines…A smart little waistcoat sounds the chic mannish note in this trim tailor-made [skirt suit]'.[52] 'Mannish' clothing at this time has been linked to the rise in sportswear and leisurewear, and, during the following decade, it appeared in the popular press as a fashion trend rather than a symbol of sexuality or subculture.[53] Hall's style fused contemporary fashions with markers of her sexual identity to forge an image of chic modernity.

In 1931 Amelia Earhart became the first president of the
'Ninety-Nines' organization of women pilots. This ushered
in an unprecedented decade of female aviation in which
women set speed and solo flying records, and beat male
pilots in pivotal air races. Names such as Amy Johnson and
Beryl Markham garnered celebrity status and, in Hollywood,
coveted aviatrix roles went to such stars of the day as
Katharine Hepburn and Kay Francis. Earhart set many
records and was the first female aviator to fly solo across the
Atlantic, for which she was the
first woman to receive the US
Distinguished Flying Cross.

Amelia Earhart
1897– disappeared 1937

Earhart's predilection for
wearing more practical men's flight garb had earned
her censure in the press during the 1920s. To avoid this
negative publicity, she began to take a greater interest
in fashion (a concession, of course, that no male pilot
would have to make), and in late 1933 she put her name
to a clothing collection in an early version of a celebrity
fashion line. Stocked in department stores such as Macy's
in New York and Marshall Field's in Chicago, the collection
offered sportswear for active living in practical fabrics that
were washable as well as wearable. The selling point was
a combination of comfort and style, as well as aviation
details, from the use of parachute silk to propeller-shaped

buttons. Earhart began to garner coverage in American *Vogue* for her own wardrobe as well as her designs.[54] In a sartorial turnaround, by 1935 she had been named one of the best-dressed women of the year by the Fashion Designers of America.[55] Unfortunately, the collection did not survive the retail downturn of the Great Depression and the line itself was short-lived.

Earhart and her second navigator Fred Noonan had completed three-quarters of their round-the-world trip when they vanished without a trace in July 1937. Theories, all of which are unsubstantiated, cloud her disappearance in mystery, from crash-landing and espionage to being killed on a Pacific island. Earhart represents adventure, emancipation and the romance of an unsolved disappearance: a heady blend that makes it easy to understand why fashion storytellers consistently fall in love with her. Her signature aviatrix style has subsequently featured on catwalks from Hermès to Prada.

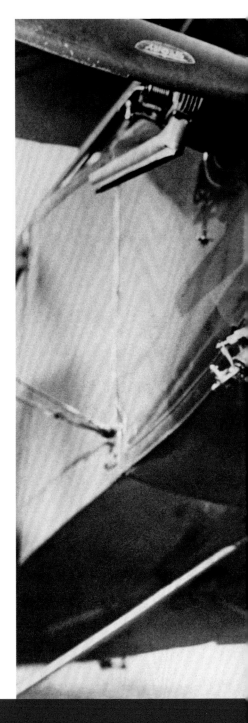

Actress Anna May Wong landed her first leading role in 1922, in one of the earliest colour feature films: *The Toll of the Sea* (Chester M Franklin). By the middle of the decade she was an international star, having played opposite Douglas Fairbanks in *The Thief of Bagdad* (Raoul Walsh, 1924). As a Chinese-American movie star, she was a pioneer of Asian Americans in Hollywood, but also a victim of the entrenched racism of cinema representations. She often missed out on leading roles to white actresses in 'yellowface', and the roles she did get often reinforced harmful and reductive stereotypes, from the subservient doomed heroine to the 'Dragon Lady'. Wong herself was aware of the limitations of her roles, saying she 'had to take what is offered'.[56]

Anna May Wong
1905–61

Much has been written about Anna May Wong's ability both on- and off-screen to use clothing to negotiate the way her own identity was portrayed through the lens of Hollywood Orientalism.[57] Studio moguls wanted her to operate as both a thoroughly modern flapper who wore the latest fashions and danced the Charleston (both of which she did very well), and as an exoticized symbol of Eastern allure. She mixed contemporary American and European looks with cheongsams brought back from a trip to China in 1936. For this she was feted by the fashion industry, who also saw her Chinese heritage as a gateway to the 'exotic'.

She was photographed by Edward Steichen for American *Vogue*, declared the 'best-dressed woman in the world' by the Mayfair Mannequin Society of New York in 1934, and pronounced the 'world's most beautiful Chinese girl' by *Look* magazine in 1938. The imagined polarity between Eastern and Western dress is expressed in *Harper's Bazaar* in November 1935. Wong wore a Lilly Daché turban, and the article notes: 'Anna May Wong's particular beauty is suited to both hemispheres. Sometimes she dresses like a Manchu princess in tight little jackets and skirts of Chinese silk, sometimes in the height of Western chic.'[58]

Anna May Wong's legacy has been long-lasting. In 1973 the Asian Fashion Designers group acknowledged her influence on fashion by naming its annual award after her.[59] She was also singled out as an inspiration by American *Vogue* in advance of the Metropolitan Museum of Art's 2015 exhibition 'China: Through the Looking Glass', which considered the impact of Chinese aesthetics on Western fashion.[60]

'Anna May Wong's particular beauty is suited to both hemispheres.'

Josephine Baker

1906–75

A star of stage and screen, Josephine Baker came from St Louis, Missouri, and caused a sensation with her 'danse sauvage' in the nightclubs of Paris in the 1920s. During her stint at the Folies Bergère she first wore her famed banana skirt, conceived initially by Jean Cocteau. The image of Baker in bananas was immortalized by the artist Paul Colin, and is as recognizeable now as it was nearly a century ago. Baker was also an activist throughout her life. She spoke at the 1963 March on Washington, and during World War II she worked as an honourable correspondent (counterespionage agent), receiving a Medal of Resistance for her work.

Baker's early stage performances forged an image of the colonial 'other' for European audiences that equated African heritage with primitivism. Her performances at this time have been read in the context of French colonialism as well as the rise of Modernism, which saw 'primitive' art as a major influence on art movements in Paris from Cubism to Art Deco.[61] Baker became simultaneously the height of Parisian chic and a symbol of fashionable exoticism.

Top designers of the day clamoured to dress her, from Jean Patou and Edward Molyneux to Madeleine Vionnet and Paul Poiret.[62] Her later years in cabaret saw her adorned in custom pieces from Dior, Lanvin, Balmain and Balenciaga.[63] Baker sparked numerous fashions in interwar Europe. Hosiery shades were named after her,[64] and later in life she claimed that vogues for short hair, coloured nail polish and suntans could all be attributed to her.[65] Baker's impact was not only felt on fashion and beauty. Alexander Calder created sculptures based on her form, and Adolf Loos even designed a house in which to 'display' her.[66] Her image was used to sell a range of products, from holidays to dolls and recipes, including her own branded hair brilliantine and skin lotion, Bakerfix and Bakerskin.[67]

Nearly two decades after Baker's death, the power of her image was harnessed yet again in a Macy's campaign that saw six windows of the department store come to life with models wearing Baker costumes from an HBO film of her life.[68] As one of the first international African–American stars, Baker continues to influence artists from Beyoncé to Miuccia Prada.

The breakdown of Mughal rule on the Indian subcontinent and increasing domination by the East India Company led to the British Raj: colonial rule in India that was established in 1858. Jawaharlal Nehru was a key figure in the resulting independence movement, headed by Mahatma Gandhi, fighting for self-rule and an end to Imperialism. Consequently, Nehru was the first prime minister of independent India from 1947 until his death in 1964. His prime-ministerial garb was distinctive and took the form of an *achkan* or *sherwani* (lapel-less jackets with a high collar) with a rose in the buttonhole and a 'Gandhi cap'. Based on the Kashmiri cap, the Gandhi cap was made from cotton rather than wool, specifically khadi cloth. Gandhi wore this style from 1919 in an attempt to unify headgear in India, and crucially he advocated the material as part of his campaign for self-rule.

Khadi was cotton cloth that was hand-spun and woven at home. The British sold cotton cloth manufactured in Manchester to the Indian subcontinent, a move that

weakened local workers and intensified India's financial dependence. Gandhi began weaving around 1915 and promoted the craft as a crucial non-violent method for resisting British rule as well as providing employment and self-sufficiency. Simple white khadi became the defining symbol of the independence movement.[69] Nehru called khadi 'the livery of freedom',[70] and in Gandhi's words: 'Khadi is the symbol of self-help, self-reliance and freedom not merely of individuals or groups, sects or clans, but of the whole nation.'[71]

The *achkan* or *sherwani* favoured by Nehru took on a life of its own in the 1960s in a shortened version: the eponymous Nehru jacket. It made particular waves in the late 1960s, when a spate of articles in the American press charted its rise to dominance in the male wardrobe, inspired in part by the growing Indian influence on countercultural styles and by The Beatles' collarless Pierre Cardin suits earlier in the decade.[72] George Frazier, a writer at *Esquire* who is often credited with popularizing the term 'peacock revolution', wrote in 1968, 'Not the least of one's reasons for not succumbing to the Nehru jacket is that hardly anyone wears it as Nehru did — beautifully tailored, unostentatious, and always with a fresh rosebud at the neck.'[73]

Jawaharlal Nehru
1889–1964

A prolific collector of 20th-century art works, Peggy Guggenheim was described by *Vogue* as, 'perhaps the most significant patron of American art'.[74] Born into the wealthy Guggenheim family, her father was a businessman who drowned on the Titanic in 1912. Her uncle set up the Solomon R Guggenheim Foundation in 1937, and later the accompanying museums. Peggy established galleries to showcase her collections, first Guggenheim Jeune in London, and later Art of This Century in New York, which was designed by architect Frederick Kiesler to house Surrealist and Abstract Expressionist works against a suitably radical backdrop. The shows she put on included some of the first exhibitions dedicated to female artists. After World War II, Guggenheim moved to the Palazzo Venier dei Leoni on the Grand Canal in Venice, where her collection is still on public display.

Peggy Guggenheim
1898–1979

Guggenheim conducted public affairs with numerous men from artistic and literary circles, challenging bourgeois notions of morality while becoming a powerful and respected woman in the male-dominated art world. 'I loved falling in love,' she told *Women's Wear Daily* (*WWD*), 'And only occasionally did I spoil it by getting married.'[75]

In her youth in Paris, Guggenheim wore couture by the likes of Jean Patou, Lucien Lelong and Charles Worth, and painted her lips bright red in a shade called 'Eternal Wound'.[76] She was photographed by Man Ray in a gown by her favourite designer Paul Poiret, paired with a headdress by Vera Stravinsky. Guggenheim's flair for the avant-garde was still evident later in her life when she was photographed in 1979 for *WWD* in an old Fortuny pleated gown and antique earrings.[77]

For much of her life, Guggenheim preferred to spend her money on her art collection rather than fashion, yet she was adept at combining the two, turning her wardrobe into wearable art. Her trademark butterfly sunglasses were designed by the artist Edward Melcarth. Artist-turned-textile-designer Ken Scott was another favourite, and she had supported him by hosting his first exhibition. Most emblematic of her passion for modern art were the two pairs of earrings made for her, one by painter Yves Tanguy and the other by sculptor Alexander Calder. She wore one of each to the opening of her Art of This Century gallery, 'in order to show my impartiality between Surrealist and Abstract art'.[78]

Frida Kahlo's legacy lives on not only in her artwork, but also in her clothing. Locked away on her death by her husband Diego Rivera, her wardrobe was rediscovered fifty years later and has since been the subject of exhibitions from Mexico City to London's Victoria and Albert Museum. Kahlo's eclectic wardrobe comprises items from Guatemala, Europe, the USA and China, as well as pieces she had made by seamstresses.[79] She is best known however, for her adoption of indigenous Amerindian dress, particularly (but not exclusively) loose, embroidered huipil blouses and skirts from the ethnically diverse Zapotec area in the Isthmus of Tehuantepec. The Tehuana ensembles Kahlo wore came into being post-1850, when European fabrics were imported, and the huipil was adopted to

Frida Kahlo
1907–54

cover previously bare torsos.[80] Her Tehuana dresses, rebozo scarves and floral headpieces have been reconfigured endlessly within the fashion industry in an attempt to capture the bohemian yet melancholy aura of Kahlo herself.

Kahlo was aware of the power of clothing to convey messages, both explicit and more subtle. She painted the torso plaster casts she wore in the wake of a road accident that left her requiring spinal support (it was in recovery that she began to paint), and she embroidered sayings into the hems of her petticoats, turning her clothing into wearable art.[81] The focus on her dress is not just a 21st-century obsession. In 1938 Bertram Wolfe wrote in American *Vogue*: 'From the bright, fuzzy, woollen strings that she plaits into her black hair and the colour she puts into her cheeks and lips, to her heavy antique Mexican necklaces and her gaily coloured Tehuana blouses and skirts, Madame Rivera seems herself a product of her art, and, like all her work, one that is instinctively and calculatedly well composed.'[82]

The period following the Mexican Revolution of 1910–20 saw Tehuana clothing emerge as the 'national dress' of Mexico.[83] As such, Kahlo's wardrobe has been read as a reflection of her maternal heritage (her mother was Mexican Catholic and her father was German Jewish), and also as a means of facilitating disability after the accident that left her reliant on the support of steel and leather corsets for the rest of her life. In spite of the complexities and multiculturalism of her wardrobe, Kahlo became a symbol of post-revolutionary Mexico. Her Tehuana clothing foregrounded the celebration of pre-Hispanic communities at a time when a unified Mexican identity was sought on the international stage.

A behemoth of 20th-century fashion, Diana Vreeland became as well known for her personal style and fashion *bons mots* as for the central place she held in the American fashion media from the 1930s to the 1980s. She began her career at *Harper's Bazaar* in 1936 and became fashion editor in 1939. Her 'Why Don't You?' columns put her on the fashion map, blending Surrealist imagery with outrageous decadence that became her hallmark. An example read: 'Why Don't You... have a private staircase from your bedroom to the library with a needlework carpet with notes of music worked on each step—the whole spelling your favourite tune?'[84]

Diana Vreeland
1903–89

As editor-in-chief of American *Vogue* from 1963 until 1971, Vreeland changed the landscape of fashion media and became the archetypal fashion editor. Bill Blass called her 'the high priestess of American fashion', while Truman Capote labelled her a genius.[85] Photographer Richard Avedon said at her funeral that she 'lived for imagination ruled by discipline and created a totally new profession. Diana Vreeland invented the fashion editor.'[86] In this respect,

her legacy lives on in popular culture. Echoes of her can be found not only in the 'Think Pink' fashion editor Maggie Prescott in *Funny Face* (Stanley Donen, 1957), but also in Miranda Priestly in *The Devil Wears Prada* (David Frankel, 2006).

From 1973 until her death in 1989, Vreeland was special consultant to the Costume Institute at the Metropolitan Museum of Art, New York. Her curatorial approach was as bombastic as her editorial style. As André Leon Talley pointed out in a piece about her 1981 exhibition, 'The 18th-Century Woman': 'There are critics who find her razzle-dazzle too Broadwaylike and who claim she is too loose with historical accuracy.' Vreeland responded: 'I give attention to beauty, extract facts and create a picture. And I never have unattractive thoughts. I won't allow them.'[87]

Opinion remains divided about Vreeland's curatorial vision that placed spectacle above scholarship. However, it is undeniable that in the early 1970s the fashion exhibition as we know it today was born. Cecil Beaton at the Victoria and Albert Museum in London, and Vreeland alongside curator Stella Blum at the Costume Institute were pioneers of the mass-appeal fashion exhibition, and demonstrated that clothing was as worthy of curation and collection as the art that hung on gallery walls.[88]

The assassination of the 35th president of the United States in 1963 remains one of the most conspiracy-ridden moments in American history. Just 43 years old when he was elected president, the young politician from Massachusetts represented an affluent New England lifestyle with a wardrobe that became a hallmark of aspirational American preppy style.

JFK

1917–63

The myth persists that Kennedy single-handedly killed off the men's hat industry by refusing to wear a hat to his inauguration, an untruth as he did wear one. However, his casual approach to dress ensured that even a century after his birth he was still touted as 'arguably the most sartorially influential person to ever hold the presidency'.[89] Kennedy married Jacqueline Lee Bouvier in 1953, and together they embodied a leisured East Coast lifestyle that was frequently captured in glossy fashion magazines.[90] JFK's sartorial codes aligned themselves with ideas around democracy and simplicity, rather than the fussy aristocratic elitism associated with Europe. However, East Coast Americana still signified markers of privilege and wealth, such as an Ivy League education.

JFK's style drew on modes that were popular on many college campuses and on the shorelines of the Atlantic coast. It was a lifestyle that was synonymous with Oxford button-down shirts, Sperry Top-Siders (boat shoes), polo shirts and chinos. The 'Ivy look' grew in popularity across the country throughout the 1950s, while JFK was a US senator. Articles touting the look are evident throughout the trade press, and, in 1957, *Women's Wear Daily* noted: 'The Ivy look is now considered a basic part of tailored blouse and shirt lines.'[91] In the same year, Sears department store advertised 'campus approved styles' as part of their Ivy looks for men.

Brands that encapsulated the American Ivy look advocated clothing that was accessible, active and functional, as well as more affordable and practical than Parisian couture. Like many other companies, GANT and Ralph Lauren grew from the Seventh Avenue wholesale trade rather than the ateliers of Paris. The Ivy look has also been linked to American entrepreneurialism; JFK was a regular wearer of Brooks Brothers, which began by selling cheap ready-made clothing imported from the UK in 1818.[92] JFK's lifestyle and casual air of leisure became a defining marker of American style, and can still be felt in American brands such as J.Crew and Tommy Hilfiger.

The showman to end all showmen, star pianist Władzio Valentino Liberace was known for his candelabra and his rhinestones, feathers, furs and lamé: the pinnacle of Las Vegas splendour. Liberace embodied a particular brand of ostentatious glittering glamour, to the extent that he was awarded a giant 22.7kg (50lb) crystal by Swarovski for services to sparkle. At the height of his fame in the 1950s and early 1960s he was receiving on average eleven thousand fan letters a week, and could draw a television audience of thirty-five million.[93] Never short of a quip regarding his opulence, he often remarked on stage, 'Pardon me while I go slip into something more spectacular.'

Liberace
1919—87

From the mid-1970s Liberace worked with costume designer Michael Travis, who also designed for Diana Ross and the Supremes, Nancy Sinatra and Dionne Warwick. Travis studied fashion in Paris before working under costume designer Edith Head in Los Angeles. They created jewel-encrusted capes with matching boots, sparkling hot pants and the 'flame' costume that was not only mirrored but also featured 1,600 tiny lights for dazzling luminescence.[94]

Although Liberace never publicly acknowledged his sexuality, journalists have claimed that his costumes and ultra-camp performances helped to foster acceptance of queer identities in a public arena.[95] This has been termed the 'Liberace Effect': an example of something that is so exaggerated people overlook it, similar to a double bluff or hiding in plain sight.[96] In 1956 Liberace instigated libel proceedings against a *Daily Mirror* columnist for an article that hinted at his sexuality (homosexuality was still illegal in the UK at that time). Liberace won, in a moment of personal triumph that had damaging ramifications as it upheld the notion that to be openly gay would jeopardize the career of an entertainer.[97]

At the time of his death, Liberace was working on a licensing deal with a fur company. The collection had special features such as 'rhinestone piano buttons, silk and gold lamé linings and a white and black mink coat reminiscent of a piano keyboard'.[98] His influence can be felt on pop performances, from Elvis's gold lamé suit (inspired by Liberace)[99] to Lady Gaga arriving at the Grammy's in an egg (based on Liberace's pink Fabergé egg stage entrance). As he acknowledged in his autobiography: 'Fashions do come and go but, luckily for me, the glitter of Liberace keeps on making people happy.'[100]

In the early 1950s Marlon Brando made a series of films that capitalized on an image of blue-collar masculinity. *A Streetcar Named Desire* (Elia Kazan, 1951), *The Wild One* (Laslo Benedek, 1953) and *On the Waterfront* (Elia Kazan, 1954) catapulted him to stardom. Brando's famed method-acting techniques, learned in New York under the Stanislavski system, were in some way extended to his film costume. He reportedly supplied his own wardrobe for *The Wild One*,[101] while a New York work crew on Eighth Avenue inspired Lucinda Ballard, costume designer for *Streetcar*. She bought jeans and T-shirts and adjusted them until they were skintight.[102] For *On the Waterfront*, costume designer Anna Hill Johnstone went to the Salvation Army to buy clothes that were authentically worn and aged.[103]

When costuming for *The Men* (Fred Zinnemann, 1950), he chose 'cheap garments from the workmen's clothing racks'.[104]

Adorned in a ripped T-shirt as Stanley in *A Streetcar Named Desire*, Brando became as well known for the body beneath his clothes as for the clothing itself, embodying a new paradigm of eroticized masculinity. The emphasis on his physical attributes was acknowledged in fan magazines such as *Photoplay*, which ran a piece on 'Hollywood men of muscle', listing vital statistics and stating that Brando 'scored his most sensational hit in a thoroughly torn shirt, and his toga in "Julius Caesar" grants an excellent view of the bulging Brando biceps'.[105]

The actor's strongest sartorial legacy comes from *The Wild One*, in which he played the smouldering, leather-clad leader of the Black Rebels Motorcycle Club in a film that was considered so dangerous that it

Marlon Brando
1924–2004

Brando's dress off-screen at this time also appeared to be a portrait of studied indifference. A profile in *LIFE* magazine in 1950 noted: 'He wore clothing so disreputable that he was refused service in three doughnut-and-coffee parlours...He displayed majestic disdain for clothes...His usual attire was blue jeans and T-shirt, with a pair of scuffed-up shoes when absolutely necessary'.

was banned in the UK for 14 years. Despite the initial *New York Times* review, which highlighted the film's 'grotesque costumes',[106] the image of Brando in black leather jacket, white T-shirt and blue jeans not only encapsulated the celluloid rebel of the 1950s, but also became a uniform of postwar youth culture. Each item has subsequently entered the canon of 'fashion classics'.

Human rights activist Malcolm X is a cultural and political icon of the African diaspora.[107] A controversial figure, he advocated fighting for civil rights 'by any means necessary', in opposition to the non-violent methods of Dr Martin Luther King. He was assassinated in 1965 by members of the Nation of Islam, a group he had publicly separated from some years earlier.

Born Malcolm Little in Nebraska, he moved to Harlem as a teenager and became involved in the underworld of drug dealing, theft and pimping. He began wearing the zoot suit, a flamboyant style born on the streets and in nightclubs, as he described: '[T]he young salesman picked off a rack a Zoot suit that was just wild: sky-blue pants thirty inches in the knee and angle-narrowed down to twelve inches at the bottom, and a long coat that pinched my waist and flared out below my knees.'[108]

Malcolm X
1925–65

The exaggerated lines of the zoot suit became aligned in popular consciousness with non-white identity, predominantly African-American and second-generation Mexican-American. By flouting rationing regulations (with its excessive use of fabric) after the US entered World War II

in 1944, the zoot suit became a form of stylistic resistance to the dominant cultural values of wartime America, and marked the wearer as unpatriotic. This contributed to the Los Angeles riots between white servicemen on leave and zoot-suited youths in June 1943. Alternative readings have seen the zoot suit as a purely aesthetic choice that has been retrospectively politicized,[109] but more often it has been understood as a subcultural marker of ethnicity and subversion to mainstream white America.[110] Malcolm X detailed in his autobiography that he wore a zoot suit as part of his strategy to avoid the draft,[111] indicating a self-fashioned identity forged out of disenfranchisement from the culture of politics, alongside an innate understanding that the personal can be political.

While in prison from 1946, Malcolm Little became involved with the political and religious group Nation of Islam, at which point he changed his surname to X, to replace the name given to his forebears by white slave masters. On his release, he moved away from the zoot suit and adopted the less ostentatious, smart, single-breasted suit, trilby hat and horn-rimmed glasses that form the iconic image for which he is remembered today. He consistently negotiated his self-representation in line with his religion, his politics and his quest for liberation.

Ernesto 'Che' Guevara was an Argentine Marxist revolutionary, physician and guerrilla fighter. He was a key player in the Cuban Revolution, which culminated in 1959 with the formation of a socialist state headed by Fidel Castro. Guevara became an international proponent of guerrilla warfare and was executed in Bolivia after a failed revolt. He remains a contentious figure: for some, an anti-imperial freedom fighter, for others a ruthless terrorist. However, his charisma was never in doubt, as summed up by photographer Henri Cartier-Bresson in *LIFE* magazine in 1963: 'His eyes glow; they coax, entice and mesmerize.'[112]

Che Guevara

1928—67

Guevara's clothing of olive-green fatigues and dark beret has become a template for the guerrilla warrior. The beret was pertinent because of its military connotations – strengthened by Field Marshal Montgomery in World War II – and its historic association with French and Basque working-class dress.

The most famous image of Guevara is *Guerrillero Heróico*, taken by Alberto Korda at the state funeral for victims of an explosion on a freighter in Havana harbour in 1960. Korda refused to take any royalties for the image, hoping to spread Guevara's message. It was first published in Europe the year that Guevara was killed. At his memorial rally, Fidel Castro addressed the crowd in Havana's Plaza de la Revolución facing a giant *Guerrillero Heróico* that covered five floors of an adjacent building.

The year following Guevara's death, student protests and anti-Vietnam fervour spread across Europe and the USA. An article in *Time* declared: 'Guevara-style beards have become a fad around Milan, and students in Florence have adopted Che's dark blue Basque beret as a trademark. Handkerchiefs, sweatshirts and blouses decorated with his shaggy countenance are popular in half a dozen countries.'[113] *Guerrillero Heróico* was given Pop Art treatment by Jim Fitzpatrick, and it is often this version that is reproduced on the T-shirts seen on people from Prince Harry to Jay-Z.

Jean Paul Gaultier used Guevara's likeness to sell sunglasses, Gisele Bündchen modelled a bikini covered in his image in 2002, and Karl Lagerfeld showed sequin berets for the Chanel Resort 2017 show held in Havana. Guevara's image has become the ultimate marker of 'radical chic', an empty symbol of youthful rebellion and anti-authoritarianism, stripped of the more complex political and ideological meanings of the original: an icon of the commodification of anti-capitalism.

Known as the 'Man in Black', Johnny Cash was a country music star who released a song and album using this name in 1971. The song outlines his affinity for black attire as a political statement, described in his second autobiography as 'my symbol of rebellion'.[114] He links the colour with poverty and outlaws, as an outward expression of inner mourning for men killed too early (a reference to the Vietnam War), and as his desire for social change:

'I wear the black for the poor and the beaten down,
Livin' in the hopeless, hungry side of town.'

His trademark look, described by *LIFE* magazine in 1969, included 'black button boots, dark striped trousers, riverboat gambler's vest, pinch-waist frock coat and ruffled white shirt'.[115]

Johnny Cash
1932–2003

Cash claimed he first began wearing black due to financial necessity as it was the only matching clothing he and his band owned.[116] Throughout history, black has been associated with the wealthy – black clothes were impractical for the poor as the dye was expensive and the process time-consuming. Black as a symbol of the poor only works within the context of industrialization, which adds another level of mourning to Cash's clothing: as a marker of a lost rural life, a theme that resonates in country music.

'Cowboy couturier' Nudie Cohn and his head tailor Manuel Cuevas often created Cash's trademark black suits. His look was much more sombre than that of Western stars like Roy Rogers, or the rock 'n' roll high living encapsulated in the diamanté Nudie Suit for country rock star Gram Parsons.[117] Black was a notable clothing colour for Cash as a performer, not only because it set him apart from the lineage of 'rhinestone cowboy' country stars, but also because it stood in opposition to wider men's fashions in the 1960s that were embracing bright colours.

Black clothing has garnered associations with passion and poetry since the time of Lord Byron (see page 130). In the 19th century black became the norm for menswear and was seen as a democratic leveller, in contrast to the glittering aristocratic flamboyance of *ancien régime* France. The poet Charles Baudelaire was arguably a forerunner to Cash when he noted: 'The black frock-coat and the tail-coat may boast not only their political beauty, which is the expression of universal equality, but also their poetic beauty, which is the expression of the public soul.'[118] Black remains a colour with a multitude of meanings, but its rebellion and poetry were captured on stage by Johnny Cash.

'I wear the black for the poor and the beaten down, Livin' in the hopeless, hungry side of town.'

South African singer Miriam Makeba became a political style icon in the 1950s and 1960s. She began her career in the nightclubs of apartheid-era Sophiatown, Johannesburg, singing with her band Manhattan Brothers. The music fused Xhosa and Zulu sounds with American jazz, and the matching look was sharp: tailored suits with imported Florsheim dress shoes.[119] Makeba's style was representative of the townships in which she lived, and was captured on the cover of South

Miriam Makeba

1932–2008

African *DRUM* magazine in 1957 when she wore a clinging off-the-shoulder dress that reached just below the knee. Makeba and her signature look featured in the film *Come Back, Africa* (Lionel Rogosin, 1959), a docudrama set in Sophiatown that centred on the violence of the apartheid regime. Seen as a hub of black cultural expression, Sophiatown was later razed by the government, re-zoned as a white area, and more than fifty thousand black inhabitants were violently relocated to the township of Soweto.

Makeba arrived in the USA in 1959 and was taken under the wing of the singer Harry Belafonte, who helped her to become a star in the early 1960s. She sang at Madison Square Garden for the birthday of JFK (*see* page 219) in 1962, won a Grammy Award for her album with Harry Belafonte in 1965, and was seen as a trendsetter for her clothes and hair.[120] *LIFE* magazine noted, 'almost everyone knows of Miriam Makeba, a sleek South African songbird.'[121] Makeba's criticism of the apartheid regime grew stronger after the Sharpeville Massacre of 1960, which saw protesters gunned down by police. Her passport was revoked and she was unable to return to her homeland until the fall of the regime some thirty years later. Throughout the 1960s her look shifted, incorporating more Afrocentric styles and headdresses. Her outspoken anti-apartheid position and her championing of independence for African states helped cement her marketed image as 'Mama Africa.'[122]

In 1968 Makeba married Stokely Carmichael, a prominent leader in the Black Power Movement. Believing his activism to be extremist, the FBI opened a file on Makeba and her American career was derailed.[123] Makeba and Nina Simone, who increasingly used her music to protest segregation and promote Civil Rights during the 1960s, have been cited as inspiration for designers Jean Paul Gaultier and Duro Olowu. In Olowu's words, they 'made considered style choices that remain potent contemporary tools of expression.'[124]

In just over a decade, Barbara Hulanicki and Stephen Fitz-Simon succeeded in embedding their shop Biba firmly within the hearts and memories of a generation of consumers. Starting out as a fashion illustrator, Hulanicki first sold her designs through a small mail-order business that advertised in newspapers such as the *Daily Mirror*. Demand was overwhelming, and, in 1964, the first Biba store opened in a former chemist in Kensington, London. Rapidly outgrowing the space, the shop moved to bigger premises the following year, and again in 1969. In 1973 they took over the 1930s department store Derry & Toms to open 'Big Biba'. Epitomizing the theatre of retail, Art Deco fantasies were enacted among giant mushrooms, Egyptian-style changing rooms and lashings of leopard print, complete with flamingos on the roof garden.

Barbara Hulanicki
b.1936

Biba is often cited as an early example of the 'designer lifestyle'. Its trademark black-and-gold logo was found on everything from pet food to baked beans. This was noted in *Men's Wear* magazine in September 1973, which stated somewhat critically: 'Biba is selling a lifestyle before it's selling clothes'. It had also come to symbolize the meritocracy of the decade, which is a significant part of the mythology of the 1960s. Clientele consisted of not only the working-class 'Biba girl', but also young aristocrats and celebrity shoppers including Twiggy, Cathy McGowan, Julie Christie, Sandie Shaw and Cilla Black.[125]

Two years after Biba opened its doors in Kensington, the London boutique boom, which had been building since Mary Quant opened Bazaar in 1955, was international news. In April 1966 *TIME* magazine ran a cover that declared London 'The Swinging City', 'a city steeped in tradition, seized by change, liberated by affluence – in a decade dominated by youth, London has burst into bloom. It swings, it is the scene.' The same article named Biba 'the most *in* shop for gear'. The next month American *Vogue* focused on London's boutiques as, 'where it all began… They've created the look that has stamped LONDON forever on the fashion map',[126] Biba was again included in their roll call. When Big Biba closed its doors in 1975, the economic boom of the 'Swinging Sixties' had morphed into a period of high inflation and industrial strikes, a climate that gave birth to Punk as the next manifestation of youth style on the streets of London.

American actress and novelist Marsha Hunt shot to fame in the UK thanks to her small role in the West End production of the musical *Hair*. On moving to London in 1966, Hunt fell straight into the heart of 'Swinging London', and one of her first jobs was babysitting for Alice Pollock, who ran the Quorum boutique that stocked Ossie Clark and other young London designers. This connection proved helpful when she embarked on her career as a singer.

Marsha Hunt
b.1946

'I decided to put an image together and asked Alice and Ossie to lend me an outfit from the Quorum boutique to go with my Vidal Sassoon haircut, false eyelashes, big red plastic hoop earrings, red pumps...and I was away.'[127]

In 1968 Hunt auditioned for the countercultural musical *Hair* that was transferring to London from Broadway. The show had an anti-Vietnam War message and featured drug taking and nudity. It opened the day after the Lord Chamberlain abolished theatre censorship, making the very brief nude scene both permissible and newsworthy. In her 1986 autobiography, Hunt credits her trademark Afro hairstyle to the London rain. She had embraced 'natural' hairstyles since a straightening incident had led to patches of her hair falling out. She was also a champion of the political connotations of the look: the Afro had developed earlier in the decade from unprocessed hairstyles linked to soul style and Black Power consciousness.[128] At the audition, she was asked to return after lunch. An hour spent in the damp climate turned her styled soft curls into tighter curls with much more volume. She was recalled and asked to keep her hairstyle the same.[129]

After the opening of the musical, *Queen* magazine featured Hunt on the cover in December 1968, her hair adorned with Christmas baubles. This was the first time that a black model had appeared on the cover of *Queen*, just two years after Donyale Luna had broken the same ground at British *Vogue*, and six years before Beverly Johnson would do the same for the American edition. The following month, Hunt graced the pages of American *Vogue*. Shot by Patrick Lichfield, the piece enthused: 'What's that there Marsha's doing with her hair? She's Naturalized it. Let it go straight. Which means, in its case, it does its thing. Goes curly, kinky, frizzy; stands, with brushing, in a seven-inch halo.'[130]

A radical Nigerian musician and pioneer of Afrobeat, Fela Anikulapo Kuti was inspired by his ancestral Yoruba culture in his dress as well as his music. He felt animosity towards corrupt political and military elites and used his songs to denounce the Nigerian government and other powerful groups and corporations, for which he was targeted by the authorities throughout his life. He founded the cooperative commune Kalakuta Republic, which he declared independent from the Nigerian government. By 1973 his international reputation was growing, as noted in American *Ebony* magazine: 'It should be stated that Fela Ransome-Kuti is, without a doubt, the West African equivalent of James Brown.'[131]

The way Fela Kuti dressed was an extension of his protest, rejecting westernized styles that he linked with oppressive colonial regimes. He often performed topless or in elaborately patterned matching tops and bottoms or jumpsuits. At times he would conduct interviews in his underwear, reportedly made by his personal tailor, another subversive act intended to undermine postcolonial westernization.[132] These elements found their way into his song lyrics, for example, the 1973 album *Gentleman* critiques what he saw as the middle-class and government obsession with Western dress.[133]

Fela Kuti
1938—97

Fela Kuti, his Afrocentric politics and his flamboyant style continue to influence the world of fashion, especially contemporary Nigerian design. Designer and artist Buki Akib launched her label in 2010 after graduating from Central Saint Martins in London with a collection named 'Fela'. She incorporates features such as handwoven Yoruba cloth called *aso oke* into her pieces.[134] Nigerian brand Kancky designed the 'Road To Kalakuta' collection for Resort 2016, which mixed Yoruba elements such as *adire* (indigo resist-dyed cloth) with bell-bottom silhouettes reminiscent of the 1970s.[135]

Buki Akib subsequently created a bag collection that was handwoven in Nigeria and inspired by Fela Kuti's 27 wives, musicians and dancers whom he married in a single ceremony and later divorced. Often pictured adorned with beads, headwraps, Ankara prints (*see* page 258) and Yoruba body art, these women have become icons of Afrocentric beauty with a global reach. As singer Solange Knowles told *Glamour* magazine: 'The Fela Kuti Queens—the band members and wives of the late African musician Fela Anikulapo Kuti—are my fashion icons.'[136]

A 2013 poll saw David Bowie crowned the best-dressed Briton in history.[137] Bowie's breakthrough came with his introduction of Ziggy Stardust in 1972. Ziggy only existed for about 18 months until the fateful night in July 1973 at the Hammersmith Odeon, when the announcement of Ziggy's retirement left fans in tears. But Ziggy's impact was phenomenal, arguably changing the look of the rock star forever.

David Bowie
1947–2016

Ziggy Stardust's look was inspired by Japanese designer Kansai Yamamoto, who staged his first fashion show in the UK in 1971 on the King's Road, London, to rave reviews in such magazines as *Harper's & Queen*, *Honey*, *Nova* and *The Sunday Times Magazine*.[138] The coverage in *Harper's & Queen* proved to be especially influential and ran with the coverline, 'Explosion from Tokyo: The fantastic sculpture clothes of a fashion architect', describing the show as 'a spectacular coup de théâtre'.[139]

Twenty years later, Bowie reminisced in the same magazine about seeing Yamamoto's reviews. He noted: 'I found all the Ziggy clothes and nearly all the look on those pages. I had the clothes copied because they were out of my league – the boots were £28 I remember; so I had the local boot-maker in Bromley make me up an identical pair...for £8 or £9.' In 1973 he met Yamamoto while on tour in Japan, who 'presented me with virtually an entire wardrobe because he knew I was wearing copies of his stuff and he realised Ziggy was becoming very popular.'[140]

Bowie also gleaned styling tips from Yamamoto's 1971 show, including the red haircut, seen on the pages of *Honey* magazine and re-created by hairdresser Suzi Fussey, and shaved eyebrows.[141] Women in Edo Period Japan (1603–1867) used to shave their eyebrows, but the custom died out after contact with the West increased as a result of the Meiji Restoration in 1868 (*see* page 164).[142] Japanese influence ran through this period of Bowie's work. In the 1960s mime artist and choreographer Lindsay Kemp had been Bowie's mentor, teaching him about Japanese dance and theatre.[143] Yamamoto also drew on Kabuki stage techniques for his fashion show, as a later report in *Women's Wear Daily* noted: 'Fashion as theater of the absurd is Kansai's metier and it has been since his... debut in London, when Kansai crouched on stage with his mannequins, veiled in black like a Kabuki stage assistant.'[144]

Ziggy only existed for about 18 months until the fateful night in July 1973 at the Hammersmith Odeon, when the announcement of Ziggy's retirement left fans in tears.

A Congolese musician and singer known as the King of Rumba Rock, Papa Wemba (Jules Shungu Wembadio Pene Kikumba) had a huge impact on both music and style. He was heralded as a key figure in the Sape movement (*Société des Ambianceurs et des Personnes Élégantes, Society of Tastemakers and Elegant People*), which takes flamboyant political and philosophical expression to a whole new level through dress and dance.

Papa Wemba
1949–2016

La Sape stretches back to the early years of colonial rule in Brazzaville (Republic of the Congo), when houseboys dressed in the cast-offs of their French masters.[145] André Grenard Matsoua, the anti-colonial politician who inspired a religion, is often credited as being the first Grand Sapeur (and is named as such in a song by Papa Wemba).[146] He returned from France in the 1920s bedecked in the latest Parisian fashions, and trips to Paris remain a mainstay of sapeur culture.[147] Yet there is also a wider history of ostentatious display in Central African dress that predates European imperialism and is closely tied to ideas of adornment, status and identity.[148] The sapeur represents an amalgam of styles, his hybridity reflecting this densely packed history.

World War II veterans returned to the area with new ideas concerning dress and democracy that would flourish into the independence movement in the following decade. At this point La Sape crossed the river into Kinshasa, capital of what is now the Democratic Republic of the Congo (DRC). DRC gained independence from Belgium in 1960, and during the 1970s President Mobutu ran 'authenticity' campaigns that banned the suit – with its associations of European imperialism – in an attempt to foster a re-Africanized national identity in a multi-ethnic region, garnering political associations for the sapeurs.[149] The pre-eminence afforded to European-style tailoring by the sapeurs was spearheaded by Papa Wemba, who popularized La Sape code with his band Viva La Musica and became a symbol of resistance to Mobutu's regime.

La Sape's *joie de vivre* contrasts vividly with continuing violent instability in the Eastern region of the DRC, fuelled by civil war at the turn of the millennium. La Sape gentlemen demonstrate savvy fashion fluency. It is not all about flashy European labels such as Versace or Gaultier, there is also a reverence for avant-garde Japanese designers including Yohji Yamamoto. Being a sapeur is much more than the sum of your wardrobe: it encompasses a distinct philosophy and, as advocated by Papa Wemba, can be a vibrant tool of political expression.

Grace Jones

b.1948

Throughout her career Grace Jones has blurred the boundaries between fashion, music and performance art, thanks to a number of creative collaborations. Graphic designer and photographer Jean-Paul Goude worked with Jones on much of her early album artwork, including the influential video for 'Slave to the Rhythm'. In 1979 Jones was pregnant with his baby. Goude, along with fashion designer Antonio Lopez, created a range of avant-garde maternity outfits for Jones, including one inspired by early 20th-century art movements Constructivism and Bauhaus. Built from angular cardboard sheets covered with coloured fabric, and accompanied by a coordinating triangular hat, the ensemble celebrated the pregnancy (she wore it to a baby shower in a nightclub), while at the same time keeping it concealed so she could still perform without the audience – or bookers – realizing she was pregnant.[150]

Yet another iconic image in 1985 saw Jones decorated with body paint by artist Keith Haring. Andy Warhol orchestrated the meeting and Haring declared: 'When I look at her, I feel her body to be the ultimate body to paint!'[151] The body art was immortalized in photographs by Robert Mapplethorpe, and later in the film *Vamp* (Richard Wenk, 1986) that saw Jones play a vampire queen adorned in Azzedine Alaïa, Issey Miyake and Haring's artwork.

Grace Jones worked as a model before she was known as a singer, and her early performances were informed and shaped by her time on the catwalk, especially her work with Issey Miyake. During her time in Paris in the mid-1970s, she auditioned for one of his shows. He taught her about Kabuki theatre, which she subsumed into her make-up, costumes and gestures on stage. In her autobiography she discusses the profound effect Miyake had on her performance style: 'He made such a contribution to how I perform, that withdrawn, minimal, underplayed performance. He showed me how to discipline the body in order to heighten the excitement...He made me realise that to make my presence felt I could stand still, and radiate intense inner life without having to dance around like all the others.' Her first public singing engagement was performing 'I Need a Man' while modelling Miyake's wedding dress for one of his end-of-show finales. Enamoured by his designs to this day, Jones claims, 'Issey is the only real artist in fashion.'[152]

A multi-instrumentalist and prolific songwriter, Prince Rogers Nelson needs no introduction. His talent and creative output can hardly be matched in the history of popular music. By the age of 18, Prince had entered the music industry and was creating what would become known as the 'Minneapolis sound'.

Prince

1958–2016

One of the first African-American stars to be played on MTV, Prince challenged dominant rules of what masculinity – especially black masculinity – should look like, and this has been considered not only in academic writing, but also in popular journalism, from the *Guardian* to *Teen Vogue*.[153] Clothing was fundamental to his stardom. An issue of *Ebony* magazine in 1985 called in experts to analyse the 'Prince Phenomenon', and his attire featured as a key point of interest. Alvin F Poussaint, Associate Professor of Psychiatry at Harvard Medical School, noted: 'His cartoon-like charisma is heightened by his ostentatious wardrobe... which gives him a mysterious satanic, messianic quality which transcends that of other performers.'[154]

'His cartoon–like charisma is heightened by his ostentatious wardrobe.'

Prince's trademark look included matching prints on suits and high-heeled shoes, buttock-baring trousers, ruffled blouses, lace and, of course, the colour purple. (My personal favourite was the cloud suit he wore in the video for his 1985 single 'Raspberry Beret', complemented by matching heeled boots.) These markers of gender nonconformity would have been at home in Louis XIV's court of Versailles (*see* page 100), where lace, extravagant neck ruffles and high heels signified virility, masculinity and power. These historical details (also adopted by New Romantics during the 1980s), were key for Louis Wells and Marie France, the costume designers for Prince's film *Purple Rain* (Albert Magnoli, 1984). In an interview with *Billboard* magazine, they noted that the ruffled shirt was inspired by the 17th century and discussed the historical significance of the colour purple.[155] Associated with Roman emperors and monarchs since antiquity due to its vast expense, purple and its link to royalty was understood by Prince, and was wholly appropriate given his name and celebrity.

Prince blurred the boundaries of conventional gender distinctions and has been hailed as the vanguard of the recent move towards gender fluidity in fashion. As a fitting celebration of his influence, in 2017, the year after his death, the first ever Prince exhibition opened at the O2 Arena in London, to showcase his life's work through objects including stage outfits, instruments and handwritten song lyrics from the archives at his Paisley Park estate in Minnesota.

Born and raised in New York's Harlem, Daniel Day, better known as Dapper Dan, spent time in his youth as a minor gangster and professional gambler with a flair for dress. In 1982 he opened Dapper Dan's Boutique on 125th Street, which became the outfitter of choice for the burgeoning hip-hop scene, catering for Eric B & Rakim, Salt-N-Pepa, LL Cool J, Big Daddy Kane and KRS-One, and notorious local gangsters. Open 24 hours a day, the boutique specialized in custom-tailored 'knock-ups' (rather than knock-offs) of branded goods from the likes of Fendi, Gucci and Louis Vuitton, mixing logos with ultra-luxe furs and leathers.

Dapper Dan
b.c.1945

The idea for knock-ups had been born eight years earlier, when Day was on his second trip to Africa. In Liberia, a local tailor had run up some leisure suits for him in vibrant local fabrics, marrying West African patterns with an American silhouette.[156] Day began by buying garment bags from Gucci stores and using their double-G leather panels for trims. Eventually he created his own silk-screen system for producing as much logo-covered leather as he could sell. Brands were not doing all-over logo clothing so Day filled this niche in the logo-obsessed 1980s, even diversifying into branded car upholstery.[157] In 2013 *The New Yorker* surmised that he was the most influential haberdasher in New York in the 1980s.[158]

The authorities were alerted to Day's unconventional retail methods in the late 1980s, following a highly publicized altercation at his store in the middle of the night between boxers Mike Tyson and Mitch 'Blood' Green. In 1992 the Fendi lawyers closed in, and Day was forced to shut up shop.

A subcultural phenomenon since the 1980s, Dapper Dan found himself counterfeited by the world of high fashion in 2017. Mainstream culture had finally caught up. After the Gucci Resort 2018 collection had been shown in Florence, Olympic runner Diane Dixon took to social media to criticize a jacket that bore a distinct resemblance to one created for her by Day in 1989. Two years earlier, Day had told *Interview* magazine that the Diane Dixon jacket was one of his favourite creations.[159] In the Gucci collection, creative director Alessandro Michele played on bootleg culture and branding, as Sarah Mower noted for *Vogue*, 'there is playfulness and conscious self-parody going on now'.[160] Proving that fashion truly is cyclical, Gucci announced a collaboration with Day in September 2017, reopening his store complete with the official use of Gucci fabrics.[161]

RuPaul

b.1960

RuPaul Andre Charles is credited with bringing drag into the mainstream with his Emmy-winning television series *RuPaul's Drag Race*. His burgeoning drag empire also includes 14 studio albums and a drag convention, and saw him land on *Time*'s list of '100 Most Influential People' in 2017.

Known for the catchphrase 'You're born naked and the rest is drag', Charles began his drag career in Atlanta, Georgia with a more unconventional look, as he recounted to Oprah Winfrey: 'It was very different from the kind I do now—it was punk rock, with combat boots and smeared lipstick.'[162] Moving to New York in the late 1980s and stepping up the glamour, he appeared in The B-52s 'Love Shack' video and went on to release his own album *Supermodel of the World* in 1993. Just three years earlier, Peter Lindbergh's seminal cover for British *Vogue* heralded the era of supermodel domination, presenting Linda Evangelista, Christy Turlington, Tatjana Patitz, Naomi Campbell and Cindy Crawford in monochrome minimalism.

RuPaul's performances both parodied and celebrated the world of high fashion. He drew on the underground culture of Harlem drag balls in the African-American and Latino gay and transgender communities, which featured in Jennie Livingston's documentary *Paris Is Burning* (1990). When MAC cosmetics launched its Viva Glam lipstick in 1994, it chose RuPaul for its first campaign, using the tagline, 'I am the MAC girl'.

The series *RuPaul's Drag Race* launched in 2009. In it, men and transgender women compete to become 'America's next drag superstar', undertaking a succession of challenges. There continues to be much crossover with the fashion world. Marc Jacobs was a guest judge on the show and cast contestant Dan Donigan, also known as Milk, in his Spring/Summer 2016 campaign. In 2015 the 'Fashion Underground: The World of Susanne Bartsch' exhibition opened at the Museum at the Fashion Institute of Technology in New York. Hailed as the queen of New York City nightlife, Bartsch gave RuPaul his big break at her experimental club-night parties in the 1980s.

Now spending more time out of drag than in it, Charles also appreciates menswear. His bespoke suits, from Los Angeles brand Klein Epstein & Parker, have custom labels that read 'Born Naked' under the collar and 'The Rest Is Drag' inside.[163]

Yinka Shonibare

b.1962

A Royal Academician and former Turner Prize nominee, Yinka Shonibare was born in London and raised in Lagos, Nigeria. Shonibare returned to the UK as a student to study fine art. The multidisciplinary artist explores race and class, and 'questions the meaning of cultural and national definitions'.[164] He does this succinctly through his use of 'African' fabrics purchased in London markets.

Closely associated with West Africa, these vivid textiles go by a number of names: Dutch wax print, Veritable Java print and Ankara, to name a few. They are derived from wax-resist fabrics. Resist-dyeing is an ancient process that flourished as batik in Indonesia, where it became a much admired art form.

The Dutch colonization of Indonesia led to the industrialization of the process in an attempt to sell manufactured batik back to Indonesia. Selling 'local' fabrics to colonized markets was big business in Europe from the 18th century; creating cloth for export could sustain whole companies in the UK or the Netherlands in the wake of the Industrial Revolution.

In the renamed 'Dutch East Indies', industrially produced batik made in Europe was seen as inferior to local handcrafted products, leaving the Dutch in need of a new export market. There is some debate over how West Africa became this new market. It is possible that Dutch ships loaded with batiks bound for Indonesia stopped at ports along the northwest coast of Africa, leading to increased demand. Another theory is that African soldiers stationed in Indonesia took batik cloth home with them, which sparked interest. Whether through trade or war, the market for batik-style prints grew enormously.[165]

Until the mid-20th century the majority of these prints were produced in Europe and sold to markets in Africa. With the independence of many African countries in the 1960s, local manufacturing grew, and the textiles, often now manufactured in China, became aligned with African identity.

Through the use of textiles in his work, Shonibare communicates complex histories, demonstrating how colonization is woven into the fabric of material culture and diasporic identities. He has also explored the idea of the dandy within this context.[166] His juxtaposition of batik-style fabrics to create 18th-century silhouettes, or the sails of Nelson's ship (Fourth Plinth, 2010),[167] embeds Africa – the root of European and American wealth through colonization and slavery – back into narratives about the UK's imperial past.

Global pop icon Beyoncé Knowles-Carter shot to fame in the late 1990s with R&B girl group Destiny's Child, and her later solo career and business empire have seen her feature on the *Forbes* list of 'The World's 100 Most Powerful Women'. Since releasing her fifth album, *Beyoncé*, in 2013, Knowles-Carter has made creative decisions that have been interpreted by many as a growing political awakening. '***Flawless', a single from the album, sampled Nigerian writer Chimamanda Ngozi Adichie's speech 'We Should All be Feminists' (*see* page 271). And the video to accompany the release of the single 'Formation' in February 2016 explicitly referenced both the Black Lives Matter movement, which has grown in response to police brutality in the USA, and Hurricane Katrina, which disproportionately affected the black community in New Orleans. The day after the single's release, Beyoncé performed the song live at the Super Bowl with her

Beyoncé b.1981

Since releasing her fifth album, *Beyoncé*, in 2013, Knowles–Carter has made creative decisions that have been interpreted by many as a growing political awakening.

troupe of dancers styled as members of the Black Panther Party. Two months later, her full visual album *Lemonade* premiered, and became the highest-selling album of the year.[168]

Beyoncé's decision to engage with these themes in her work has been celebrated for increasing the representation of black women in pop culture, joining a lineage of black protest musicians, and introducing fans to Civil Rights history, as well as folk elements from Yoruba culture and the American South.[169] However, prominent social activist bell hooks, whose work looks at the intersections between class, race and gender, has been publically critical of Beyoncé for what she views as commodified protest, while others have condemned her for paying lip service to activism in order to sell tour tickets and merchandise.[170] The single 'Formation' is rooted in the idea that capitalism can be a means to escape oppression, and luxury fashion plays a key role in this: the lyrics cite Givenchy, while customized and new-season Gucci is worn. The styling throughout *Lemonade* creates visual spectacle and stunning imagery that looks entirely modern while referencing antebellum silhouettes. The yellow Roberto Cavalli dress that features in the single 'Hold Up', accessorized with a baseball bat, spawned countless 'get the look' features.[171]

Despite using luxury labels in her videos, Beyoncé has made her own ventures into fashion much more accessible. Her first foray into the industry was House of Deréon, the ready-to-wear label that grew from her mother's creations for Destiny's Child.[172] The latest line, activewear brand Ivy Park, heralds the unstoppable rise of athleisure in the 21st-century market. A partnership with Topshop, Ivy Park debuted in April 2016 marrying sport and street styles with a fashion-conscious aesthetic.

Iris Apfel

b.1921

Self-proclaimed 'geriatric starlet' Iris Apfel first came to global attention at the age of 83, when the Metropolitan Museum of Art's Costume Institute in New York staged an exhibition of her accessories and fashion in 2005. Harold Koda curated 'Rara Avis: Selections from the Iris Apfel Collection', choosing the exhibition title because, 'Even in the flock of New York style setters, she stands apart as a rare bird.'[173]

Known for her bold and eclectic look that eschews fashion trends in favour of personal style, Apfel mixes couture with flea-market finds, historic and antique garments, and handcrafted pieces picked up on her travels. She has been involved in numerous fashion campaigns and collaborations with, for example, MAC Cosmetics, Macy's department store, Jimmy Choo, Kate Spade and even a range of wearable tech.[174] Her influence has reached outside the world of fashion, with Apfel claiming, 'I've been accused of liberating and inspiring hordes of women of every age to have more courage in dressing and not to be afraid of experimentation.'[175] Throughout her working life, Apfel and her husband ran an interior-design business called Old World Weavers that specialized in creating reproductions of historic fabrics. Their clients extended to the White House, through nine presidencies. They used to travel for months at a time to source mills and fabrics, which also provided inspiration for Apfel's wardrobe. Her father had worked for Elsie de Wolfe, the extravagant celebrity interior designer, whose personal style and synergy between interiors and fashion impacted Apfel and her approach later in life.

Celebrated filmmaker Albert Maysles captured Apfel's life in his penultimate film, *Iris* (2014). Filmed over four years, the documentary features such designers as Duro Olowu and Dries Van Noten, who have been inspired by Apfel's style. Some forty years earlier, Maysles introduced the world to another idiosyncratic dresser-turned-muse, Little Edie (Edith Bouvier Beale), who became a perennial source of fashion inspiration following his documentary *Grey Gardens* (1975).

Despite the flamboyance of Apfel's accessorizing, she claims that jeans remain a constant favourite for her as they act as a canvas on which to build an outfit. In her own words, 'Wit and humour are key components to my philosophy of dressing. Never take yourself or an outfit too seriously.'[176]

It is not unusual for American politicians to send political messages through clothing. As *Business of Fashion* pointed out, Barack Obama often employed Brooklyn-based tailor Martin Greenfield to make his suits, supporting US industry,[177] and Madeleine Albright used brooches to communicate diplomatic intentions during her time at the United Nations.[178] However, the First Lady occupies a particular place in American politics, where the symbolism of dress takes on a heightened role as a form of diplomacy on the global and domestic stage. This is so embedded in American culture that the Smithsonian's National Museum of American History has a 'First Ladies Collection', asking each First Lady to donate a garment that represents them.

Michelle Obama

b.1964

Obama rewrote the First Lady stylebook with a mix of more affordable brands, established and up-and-coming American designers, supporting domestic business while retaining an air of inclusivity through her choice of brands such as JCrew and Gap alongside Calvin Klein, Narciso Rodriguez, Michael Kors, Thakoon and Isabel Toledo. She wore gowns by New York-based Jason Wu to both inauguration balls, catapulting him to international prominence.

During the economic downturn that followed the financial crash of 2008,[180] Obama was praised for the pragmatism and 'relatability' of her clothing choices. She has won plaudits from the fashion industry, which included three *Vogue* covers, and a special tribute award from the Council of Fashion Designers of America (CFDA) in 2009. CFDA president Diane von Furstenberg noted her 'meteoric rise as a fashion icon'.[181]

As the country's only African–American First Lady, hailing from Chicago's South Side, Michelle Obama broke down barriers in this position that had previously been dominated by the wealthy and white. A Princeton-educated career woman and mother who can trace her ancestry back to slaves and slave owners, Obama embodied not only the American Dream, but also fundamental aspects of American history and its legacy.[179]

The originality of Obama's choices often spark comparisons to Jackie Kennedy, the archetypal First Lady who continues to dominate 'style icon' lists.[182] However, as former *Vogue* editor-at-large André Leon Talley pointed out, Obama's practical fashion choices and progressive agenda are more in line with Eleanor Roosevelt who shared her passion and support for human rights.[183]

Conceptual artist Yayoi Kusama has been creating works of sculpture, fiction, painting, performance, film and installation since the 1950s. She has exhibited around the globe,

Yayoi Kusama
b.1929

with major retrospectives at the Whitney Museum of American Art in New York and Tate Modern in London, as well as an eponymous museum in Tokyo. Kusama is well known for her use of polka dots, which she claims represent the human condition: 'Polka dots must always multiply to infinity. Our earth is only one polka dot among millions of others.'[184] Kusama moved to New York in 1957 and was involved in the avant-garde art world throughout the following decade, where her 'happenings' featured naked participants painted with polka dots.

Kusama has long been interested in breaking the boundaries between art and fashion. In the 1960s, her collections under the banner Kusama Fashion Company Ltd included transparent dresses with polka dots, dresses with strategically placed holes, metallic dresses covered with florals, and shoes with phallic protrusions, some of which were available at the 'Kusama Corner' at Bloomingdales.[185] In 2012 Kusama was again working in high fashion in partnership with

Louis Vuitton, in Vuitton's most extensive artist collaboration to date. Vuitton sponsored a number of Kusama's exhibitions and produced a collection that included clothing, shoes, sunglasses, watches and leather goods all in her signature polka-dot prints.

There is a strong synergy between the worlds of fashion and art that stretches back to at least Elsa Schiaparelli and Salvador Dali's Surrealist designs of the 1930s. With Marc Jacobs at the helm, Louis Vuitton embraced the potential for relationships across these fields, infusing luxury goods with added cultural capital. It began in 2001 with artist Stephen Sprouse, followed by illustrator Julie Verhoeven, and then, in 2003, by contemporary artist Takashi Murakami. These collections brought a contemporary and collectable element to the heritage luggage brand best known for its monogram.[186] The Kusama collections came from a meeting with Marc Jacobs in 2006. Kusama stated that Jacob's attitude towards art was the same as her own: 'I respect him as a wonderful designer. Louis Vuitton understands and appreciates the nature of my art. Therefore there isn't much difference from my process of making fashion.'[187] The collaboration with Vuitton underscored Kusama's ability throughout her career to successfully interweave high art, performance and fashion.

Chimamanda Ngozi Adichie
b.1977

Nigerian writer Chimamanda Ngozi Adichie is an award-winning novelist who has also penned short stories and nonfiction. In 2012 Adichie gave a TEDxEuston talk titled 'We Should All Be Feminists', which has since been published as an essay.[188] The talk came to greater international attention after it was sampled by Beyoncé (see page 261) on her 2013 single '***Flawless'. Adichie has since distanced herself from Beyoncé's form of feminism,[189] but the single helped to expand Adichie's literary recognition and cement her fame as a global icon of intersectional feminism.

Adichie's message entered the popular arena yet again when Maria Grazia Chiuri, the first ever female creative director at Dior, emblazoned it on T-shirts as part of the house's Spring/Summer 2017 collection in Paris. Chiuri's inaugural Dior collection was significant because it challenged the historical all-male directorship of the house. It was accompanied by a pre-show statement that celebrated Adichie's work 'examining the question of racism and the place of women in society'.[190] A focus on feminism in fashion grew throughout the 2010s. Karl Lagerfeld came under criticism for co-opting the aesthetics of feminism in a Chanel show that saw models storm the catwalk finale with faux-feminist banners.[191]

In the wake of the Women's March of 2017, in which protesters took to the streets across the world in opposition to Donald Trump's presidency, Angela Missoni created her own version of the Pussyhat, the knitted pink hat that became a symbol of the march. Some proceeds were donated to civil liberties and refugee charities.[192]

With a lifelong interest in clothing – 'If I had a style mantra it was to wear what I liked' – Adichie has talked of her negotiations between fashion and intellectual public life, decrying the manufactured division between the two. She continues to make statements through her clothing with 'Project Wear Nigerian', which prioritizes Nigerian designers for public engagements and is documented on an Instagram profile run by her nieces. Adichie wrote in the *Financial Times*: 'I have practical hopes for my project, that it shows Nigerian fashion as it is, not a museum of "traditional African" clothes but a vibrant and diverse industry, and that it brings recognition to the brands. But it is also a personal and political statement...This project is an act of benign nationalism, a paean to peaceful self-sufficiency, a gesture towards what is still possible; it is my uncomplicated act for complicated times.'[193]

Hillary Rodham Clinton was the first female nominee for US president and the winner of the popular vote in the 2016 American election. The self-proclaimed 'pantsuit aficionado' included a trompe-l'oeil pantsuit T-shirt in her campaign merchandise, and her endorsement saw a spike in pantsuit sales and a number of women donning them to vote.[194] Clinton fully embraced the pantsuit when she ran for senate in 2000 and during her first bid for presidential nominee in 2008.[195] The pantsuit became a marker of the ultimate attempt to smash the glass ceiling.

In her book following the election, Clinton discussed her proclivity for the pantsuit, claiming that it made her feel professional,

Hillary Rodham Clinton

b.1947

while also functioning as a uniform that was 'an anti-distraction technique: since there wasn't much to say or report on what I wore, maybe people would focus on what I was saying instead'.[196] As a woman at the frontline of politics for decades, she was aware of the criticism that could come with more daring fashion choices.[197]

During the 2016 campaign, the fashion industry overwhelmingly sided with Hillary.

Donors included Tory Burch, Michael Kors, Marc Jacobs, Prabal Gurung, Vera Wang, Calvin Klein, Diane von Furstenberg and Ralph Lauren. Supporters such as Thakoon, Jacobs and Burch also designed campaign T-shirts.[198] *Business of Fashion* reported that Anna Wintour advised Clinton on her wardrobe,[199] and Ralph Lauren created pantsuits for many of her key moments.[200]

The presidential campaign was not her first brush with fashion. As First Lady, she appeared on the cover of American *Vogue* in December 1998, photographed by Annie Leibowitz. The accompanying article noted that even in those pre-pantsuit days her clothing was intended to be fit for purpose, becoming 'a kind of uniform or habit, designed as much to deflect attention as to catch it'.[201]

Clinton wore a 'suffragette-white pantsuit'[202] at the 2016 Democratic National Convention when she was announced as the party's nominee, and again at the Trump inauguration.[203] A keen interest in suffrage history has run through Clinton's career,[204] making this a pertinent choice. As the UK suffrage newspaper *Votes for Women* wrote in 1911: 'White is especially dear, so much so that the casual passer-by may be heard to remark, "Oh! they're suffragettes, look how they're dressed," when he meets ladies clad in white'.[205]

VOGUE

ARABIA

JUNE

ALL EYES ON
HALIMA
ADEN
The runway
star shattering
stereotypes

NEW LOOK
*Past meets future
to revolutionize
your style*

CELEBRATING

Somali-American model Halima Aden made history in July 2017 in *Allure* magazine as the first hijab-wearing model to feature on the cover of a major American magazine. Aden was born in a Kenyan refugee camp after her parents fled from the Somali Civil War in the early 1990s. After the family's application was vetted, a process that took nearly a decade, they moved via St Louis, Missouri, to St Cloud, Minnesota. Aden was later elected homecoming queen and, in 2016, entered the Miss Minnesota USA pageant as the first hijabi beauty contestant.[206]

women, while right-wing groups have targeted religiously demarcated Muslim dress such as the burka as a (misplaced) symbol of fundamentalist terrorism. Halima Aden is one of a growing number of 'hijabistas' who, through blogging and representation on social media (and increasingly traditional media), are challenging preconceived notions about Muslim women. As Aden told the *Financial Times*: 'I have an opportunity, through my modelling, to change the way that Muslim women are viewed, to give them a platform to have their voices heard.'[209]

Halima Aden

b.1997

She was scouted by a model agency and subsequently walked in shows for Yeezy, MaxMara and Alberta Ferretti, wearing high-fashion, modest styles that adhered to her religious beliefs.

Aden's well-deserved success in the fashion industry comes at a time of criticism about the industry's lack of diversity, and the politicization of the hijab and other markers of Muslim dress post-9/11.[207] *Harper's Bazaar* noted that Aden was the first model to dress modestly and wear a hijab while working.[208] Some Western commentators condemn the hijab as oppressive for

Casting Aden also makes business sense. A Reuters report claimed Muslim consumer spending comprised 11 per cent of the global market in 2015 at $243 billion, set to rise to $368 billion by 2021.[210] In 2016 Dolce & Gabbana launched its first abaya collection, while Gap, Nike, Uniqlo and American Eagle have all designed lines or products with the Muslim consumer in mind. Websites such as *The Modist* sell luxury fashion that caters for a modest consumer. Such clothing, comprising looser items, longer hemlines and sleeves, and higher necks, once associated with religious dress for, among others, Christians, Jews and Muslims, has found its way into secular fashion and now appears on the style pages of the *Guardian* and *The New York Times*.[211]

Endnotes

Introduction

1. Kitchen, A., Light, J. E., Reed, D. L. and Toups, M. A. 'Origin of Clothing Lice Indicates Early Clothing Use by Anatomically Modern Humans in Africa', in *Molecular Biology and Evolution*, vol.28, issue 1, 1 January 2011: 29–32.
2. Gilligan, I. 'The Prehistoric Development of Clothing: Archaeological Implications of a Thermal Model', in *Journal of Archaeological Method and Theory*, vol.17, issue 1, March 2010: 15–80.

Ancient

1. Maxwell, E. 'Happy New Year', in American *Vogue*, 1 January 1934: 21.
2. Aldersey-Williams, H. *Anatomies: A Cultural History of the Human Body*, W W Norton & Company, 2013: 203.
3. Esquevin, C. *Adrian: Silver Screen to Custom Label*, Monacelli Press, 2007: 53.
4. See 'Voyage to Cythera' Autumn/Winter 1989–90, Spring/Summer 2011 MAN collection and the Gold Label Spring/Summer 2015 show.
5. O'Sullivan, N., Teasdale, M., et al. 'A whole mitochondria analysis of the Tyrolean Iceman's leather provides insights into the animal sources of Copper Age clothing', in *Scientific Reports*, 6, published online 18 August 2016: nature.com/articles/srep31279.
6. Krosnar, K. 'Now you can walk in footsteps of 5,000-year-old Icernan – wearing his boots', in the *Telegraph*, 17 July 2005: telegraph.co.uk/news/worldnews/europe/italy/1494238/Now-you-can-walk-in-footsteps-of-5000-year-old-Iceman-wearing-his-boots.html.
7. Barber, Elizabeth Wayland. 'On the Antiquity of East European Bridal Clothing', in *Dress: The Journal of the Costume Society of America*, vol.21, issue 1, 1994: 17–29.
8. Frei, K. M., Mannering, U., Kristiansen, K., Allentoft, M. E., Wilson, A. S., Skals, I., Tridico, S., Nosch, M. L., Willerslev, E., Clarke, L. and Frei, R. 'Tracing the dynamic life story of a Bronze Age Female', *Scientific Reports*, May 2015: nature.com/articles/srep10431; 'The Bronze Age Egtved Girl was not from Denmark', Faculty of Humanities, University of Copenhagen, 21 May 2015: humanities.ku.dk/news/2015/the_bronze_age_egtved_girl_was_not_danish/.
9. Hall, R. *Egyptian Textiles*, Shire Publications, 1986: 47.
10. Fowler, B. 'Forgotten Riches of King Tut: His Wardrobe', in *The New York Times*, 25 July 1995: nytimes.com/1995/07/25/science/forgotten-riches-of-king-tut-his-wardrobe.html.
11. Hall, R., 1986: 40; Fletcher, J. 'The Decorated Body in Ancient Egypt: Hairstyles, Cosmetics and Tattoos', in Cleland, L., Harlow, M., Llewellyn-Jones, L. (eds.) *The Clothed Body in the Ancient World*, Oxbow Books, 2005: 4.
12. Fletcher, J., 2005: 9.
13. For more, see Brier, B. *Egyptomania: Our Three Thousand Year Obsession with the Land of the Pharaohs*, Palgrave Macmillan, 2013: 161–73.
14. Corlett, D. S. 'The Kohl Pots of Egypt', in American *Vogue*, 1 September 1923: 56.
15. Von Wees, H. 'Trailing Tunics and Sheepskin Coats: Dress and Status in Early Greece', in Cleland, L., Harlow, M. and Llewellyn-Jones, L. (eds.) *The Clothed Body in the Ancient World*, Oxbow Books, 2005: 44–50; Alden, M. 'Ancient Greek Dress', in *Costume*, vol.37, issue 1, January 2003.
16. Translation from Parker, H. 'Sappho's Public World', in Greene, E. (ed.) *Women Poets in Ancient Greece and Rome*, University of Oklahoma Press, 2005: 13. See also Van Wees, H. in *The Clothed Body in the Ancient World*, 2005: 49.
17. Translation from Williamson, M. 'Sappho and the Other Woman', in Greene, E. (ed.) *Reading Sappho: Contemporary Approaches*, University of California Press, 1996: 253.
18. Lee, M. 'Constru(ct)ing Gender in the Feminine Greek Peplos', in *The Clothed Body in the Ancient World*, 2005: 60–3.
19. For more, see Koda, H. *Goddess: The Classical Mode*, Metropolitan Museum of Art, 2003.
20. Liu-Perkins, C. *At Home in Her Tomb: Lady Dai and the Ancient Chinese Treasures of Mawangdui*, Charlesbridge Publishing, 2014: 47.
21. Bonn-Muller, E. 'Entombed in Style', in *Archaeology*, vol.62, no.3, May/June 2009: 40–3.
22. Liu, X. *The Silk Road in World History*, Oxford University Press, 2010: 1, 10; Barisitz, S. *Central Asia and the Silk Road: Economic Rise and Decline over Several Millennia*, Springer, 2017: 39–40.
23. Steele, V. and Major, J. S. *China Chic: East Meets West*, Yale University Press, 1999: 55–61; Wilson, V. 'Dress and the Cultural Revolution', in *ibid*.: 167–7.
24. Gray, M. 'Poison, not snake, killed Cleopatra, scholar says', *CNN*, 30 June 2010: edition.cnn.com/2010/WORLD/europe/06/30/cleopatra.suicide/.
25. Walters, B. (trans.) *Lucan, Civil War [Pharsalia]*, Hackett Publishing, 2015: 223–6.
26. Ashton, S. A. *Cleopatra and Egypt*, John Wiley & Sons, 2008: 147.
27. See, for example, Mitchell, R. N. 'The Victorian Fancy Dress Ball, 1870–1900', in *Fashion Theory*, vol.21, issue 3, 2017: 291–315.
28. See Adler, D. 'The Unlacing of Cleopatra', in *Theatre Journal*, vol.34, no.4, December 1982: 450–66.
29. For more on fashion tie-ins for the *Cleopatra* films, see Buchart, A. *The Fashion of Film: How Cinema has Inspired Fashion*, Mitchell Beazley, 2016: 82–5.
30. Stone, S. 'The Toga: From National to Ceremonial Costume', in Sebesta, J. L. and Bonfante, L. (eds.) *The World of Roman Costume*, University of Wisconsin Press, 2001: 13.
31. Harlow, M. 'Dress in the *Historia Augusta*: the Role of Dress in Historical Narrative', in *The Clothed Body in the Ancient World*, 2005: 148.
32. Davies, G. 'What Made the Roman Toga virilis?', in *The Clothed Body in the Ancient World*, 2005: 127.
33. *Ibid.*: 125.
34. Stout, A. M. 'Jewelry as a Symbol of Status in the Roman Empire', in *The World of Roman Costume*, 2001: 82.
35. Hales, S. 'Men are Mars, Women are Venus: Divine Costumes in Imperial Rome', in *The Clothed Body in the Ancient World*, 2005: 134–5.
36. For more, see Ribeiro, A. *Fashion in the French Revolution*, Batsford Ltd, 1988.
37. Hingley, R. *Boudica: Iron Age Warrior Queen*, A & C Black, 2006: 53–4.
38. Williams, C. D. *Boudica and Her Stories: Narrative Transformations of a Warrior Queen*, University of Delaware Press, 2009: 63–4.
39. *Ibid.*: 63.
40. Rosten, J. F. 'Personal adornment and the expression of identity in Roman Britain: a study of the material culture of appearance', submitted for the award of Doctor of Philosophy (Ph.D), University of Leicester, 2007: 31.
41. Carr, G. 'Woad, Tattooing and Identity in Later Iron Age and Early Roman Britain', in *Oxford Journal of Archaeology*, vol.24, issue 3, 2005: 288.
42. *Ibid.*: 278–9.
43. See thewoadcentre.co.uk.
44. Lonsdale, S. 'Boudicca's warpaint puts farmer on the woad to recovery', 28 September 2003: telegraph.co.uk/news/uknews/1442692/Boudiccas-warpaint-puts-farmer-on-the-woad-to-recovery.html.

Medieval

1. Evans, J. A. *The Empress Theodora: Partner of Justinian*, University of Texas Press, 2003: x–xv; Garland, L. *Byzantine Empresses: Women and Power in Byzantium AD 527–1204*, Routledge, 2002: 11–16.
2. Hennessy, K. (ed.) *Fashion: The Ultimate Book of Costume and Style*, Dorling Kindersley, 2012: 36.
3. Ball, J. *Byzantine Dress*, Springer, 2005: 21; Cameron, A. 'A Byzantine Imperial Coronation of the Sixth Century AD', in *Costume*, vol.7, issue 1, 1973: 6–7.
4. Hall, R., 1986: 10; Burnard, J. *Chintz and Cotton: India's Textile Gift to the World*, Kangaroo Press, 1994: 45.
5. Prestwich, M. *Medieval People*, Thames & Hudson, 2014: 16.
6. Geary, P. J. *Readings in Medieval History: The Early Middle Ages*, University of Toronto Press, 2010: 275.
7. *Ibid.*
8. Owen-Crocker, G. R. *Dress in Anglo-Saxon England*, Boydell Press, 2004: 179.
9. *Ibid.*
10. Other suggestions have been proposed, see, for example, Bridgeford, A. 'Was Count Eustace II of Boulogne the patron of the Bayeux Tapestry?', in *Journal of Medieval History*, vol.25, issue 3, 1999; Owen-Crocker, G. R. 'The Bayeux "Tapestry": Culottes, Tunics and Garters, and the Making of the Hanging', in *Costume*, vol.28, issue 1, January 1994; Lewis, M. J. 'Questioning the Archaeological Authority of the Bayeux Tapestry', in *Cultural and Social History*, vol.7, issue 4, 2010: 467–84.
11. Owen-Crocker, G. R. 'The Bayeux "Tapestry": Culottes, Tunics and Garters, and the Making of the Hanging', in *Costume*, vol.28, issue 1, January 1994; Lewis, M. J. 'Questioning the Archaeological Authority of the Bayeux Tapestry', in *Cultural and Social History*, vol.7, issue 4, 2010: 467–84.
12. For more on this, see Parker, R. *The Subversive Stitch: Embroidery and the Making of the Feminine*, I. B. Tauris, 2013 [1984].

13. McMillan, J. 'The House That Jack Built: Essay as Sampler', foreword in Kenny, R., McMillan, J. and Myrone, M. *British Folk Art*, Tate Publishing, 2014: 13.
14. Weir, A. *Eleanor of Aquitaine: By the Wrath of God, Queen of England*, Random House, 2011: 19.
15. *Ibid.*: 36.
16. Snyder, J. 'From Content to Form: Court Clothing in Mid-Twelfth-Century Northern French Sculpture', in Koslin, D. and Snyder, J. (eds.) *Encountering Medieval Textiles and Dress: Objects, Texts, Images*, Springer, 2016: 87–9.
17. Hennessy, K. (ed.), 2012: 55.
18. Beckwith, C. I. *Empires of the Silk Road: A History of Central Eurasia from the Bronze Age to the Present*, Princeton University Press, 2011: 183.
19. Prestwich, M. *Medieval People: Vivid Lives in a Distant Landscape*, Thames & Hudson, 2014: 114.
20. McLynn, F. *Genghis Khan: The Man Who Conquered the World*, Penguin Random House, 2016: 20.
21. Komaroff, L. (ed.) *Beyond the Legacy of Genghis Khan*, BRILL, 2012: 7; McLynn, F., 2016: 20.
22. Prestwich, M., 2014: 116.
23. For more, see Komaroff, L. and Carboni, S. (eds.) *The Legacy of Genghis Khan: Courtly Art and Culture in Western Asia, 1256–1353*, Metropolitan Museum of Art and Yale University Press, 2002.
24. DeMello, M. *Feet and Footwear: A Cultural Encyclopedia*, Greenwood Press/ABC-CLIO, 2009: 159–60.
25. Gardner, J. '*Opus Anglicanum* and its Medieval Patrons', in Browne, C., Davies, G. and Michael, M. A. (eds.) *English Medieval Embroidery: Opus Anglicanum*, Yale University Press in association with the Victoria and Albert Museum, 2016: 52–3, 69–70.
26. *Ibid.*: 51–4.
27. Newton, S. M. *Fashion in the Age of the Black Prince: A Study of the Years 1340–1365*, Boydell Press, 1980: 15.
28. Barber, R. *Edward III and the Triumph of England: The Battle of Crécy and the Company of the Garter*, Penguin Books, 2013.
29. For more on the jupon and its replica, see Arnold, J. 'The jupon, or coat-armour, of the Black Prince in Canterbury Cathedral', in *Church Monuments*, vol.VIII, 1993: 12–24.
30. King James Bible, Deuteronomy 22:5.
31. Warner, M. *Joan of Arc: The Image of Female Heroism*, Oxford University Press, 2013: 129.
32. Crane, S. *The Performance of Self: Ritual, Clothing, and Identity During the Hundred Years War*, University of Pennsylvania Press, 2012: 75.
33. *Ibid.*: 74–5.
34. *Ibid.*: 85.

Early Modern

1. For more on these discussions, see Hicks, C. *Girl in a Green Gown: The History and Mystery of the Arnolfini Portrait*, Random House, 2011; and Graham, J. *Inventing van Eyck: The Remaking of an Artist for the Modern Age*, Berg Publishers, 2007.

2. Murray, J. M. *Bruges, Cradle of Capitalism, 1280–1390*, Cambridge University Press, 2005.
3. For more on Flanders and luxury, see Buylaert, F., De Clercq, W. and Dumolyn, J. 'Sumptuary legislation, material culture and the semiotics of "vivre noblement" in the county of Flanders (14th–16th centuries)', in *Social History*, vol.36, no.4, 2011: 393–417.
4. Andersson, E. I. 'Clothing and Textile Materials in Medieval Sweden and Norway', in Netherton, R. and Owen-Crocker, G. R. (eds.) *Medieval Clothing and Textiles 9*, Boydell Press, 2013: 101.
5. *The Athenaeum* no.714, 1841: 509.
6. See Kenneth Clark in Scott, M. *Late Gothic Europe, 1400–1500*, History of Dress Series, Mills & Boon, 1980: 40; 40–55 for discussion on possible reasons for this 'gothic ideal'.
7. Duchâteau, A. *Benin: Royal Art of Africa*, Prestel, 1994: 12.
8. *Ibid*: 9.
9. Okpokunu, E., Agbontaen-Eghafona, K. A. and Ojo, P. O. 'Benin Dressing in Contemporary Nigeria: Social Change and the Crisis of Cultural Identity', in *African Identities*, vol.3, issue 2, 2005: 156.
10. Ben-Amos, P. *The Art of Benin*, Thames & Hudson, 1980: 23, 68.
11. Okpokunu, E., Agbontaen-Eghafona, K. A. and Ojo, P. O. in *African Identities*, 2005: 160–3.
12. Kriger, C. E. *Cloth in West African History*, AltaMira Press, 2006: 33.
13. Ben-Amos, P., 1980: 17.
14. For more, see Okpokunu, E., Agbontaen-Eghafona, K. A. and Ojo, P. O. in *African Identities*, 2005: 155–70.
15. Grancsay, S. V. 'Maximilian Armor', in *The Metropolitan Museum of Art Bulletin*, vol.23, no.4, April 1928: 102.
16. Clifton, J. '"To showe to posteritie the manner of soldiers apparel": Arms and Armour in European Prints', in Sinkević, I. (ed.) *Knights in Shining Armor: Myth and Reality 1450–1650*, Bunker Hill Publishing, 2006: 61.
17. *Ibid.*: 62.
18. Watts, K. 'Henry VIII and the Founding of the Greenwich Armouries', in Starkey, D. *Henry VIII: A European Court in England*, Collins & Brown, 1991: 42–5.
19. 'Aztec' is a contested umbrella term, see Schreffler, M. '"Their Cortés and Our Cortés": Spanish Colonialism and Aztec Representation', in *The Art Bulletin*, vol.91, issue 4, 2009: 420.
20. Bassett, M. 'Meeting the Gods: Apotheoses and Exchanges of the Early Encounter', in *Material Religion*, vol.8, issue 4, December 2012: 416–38.
21. Anawalt. P. R. 'Costume and Control: Aztec Sumptuary Laws', in *Archaeology*, vol.33, no.1, January/February 1980: 35.
22. *Ibid.*: 33–43.
23. Anawalt, P. R. 'The Emperors' Cloak: Aztec Pomp, Toltec Circumstances', in *American Antiquity*, vol.55, issue 2, 1990: 291–307.
24. For more on this as related to Moctezuma, see Boone, E. H. 'Seeking Indianness: Christoph Weiditz, the Aztecs, and feathered Amerindians', in *Colonial Latin American Review*, vol.26, issue 1, 2017: 39–61.
25. Riedler, R., Pearlstein, E. and Gleeson, M. 'Featherwork: Beyond Decorative', in *Studies*

in Conservation, vol.57, issue sup1, 2012: S244–S249.
26. Hayward, M. 'Luxury or Magnificence? Dress at the Court of Henry VIII', in *Costume*, vol.30, issue 1, January 1996: 38–40.
27. Isaac, V. 'Presuming Too Far "above his very base and low degree"?: Thomas Cromwell's Use of Textiles in his Schemes for Social and Political Success (1527–1540)', in *Costume*, vol.45, issue 1, 2011: 8–23.
28. For more, see Orakcioglu, M., Orakcioglu, I. and Fletcher, B. C. 'Enclothed Cognition and Hidden Meanings in Important Ottoman Textiles', in *TEXTILE*, vol.14, issue 3, 2016: 360–75.
29. Mackie, L. W. 'Ottoman Kaftans with an Italian Identity', in Faroqhi, S. and Neumann, C. K. *Ottoman Costumes: From Textile to Identity*, EREN, 2004: 220.
30. Jirousek, C. 'More Than Oriental Splendor: European and Ottoman Headgear, 1380–1580', in *Dress*, vol.22, issue 1, 1995: 24.
31. Tezcan, H. 'Furs and Skins Owned by the Sultans', in Faroqhi, S. and Neumann, C. K. *Ottoman Costumes: From Textile to Identity*, EREN, 2004: 76–7.
32. Baker, P. L. 'Islamic Honorific Garments', in *Costume*, vol.25, issue 1, January 1991: 25.
33. Mansel, P. *Dressed to Rule: Royal and Court Costume from Louis XIV to Elizabeth II*, Yale University Press, 2005: 38–41.
34. Faroqhi, S. 'Introduction, or Why and How One Might Want to Study Ottoman Clothes', in Faroqhi, S. and Neumann, C. K., 2004: 22–5; Mansel, P., 2005: 38. See also Dunn, J. P. 'Clothes to Kill For: Uniforms and Politics in Ottoman Armies', in *The Journal of the Middle East and Africa*, vol.2, issue 1, 2011: 91–2.
35. Hayward, M. *Dress at the Court of King Henry VIII*, Routledge, 2017: 16–17.
36. Jirousek, C, in *Dress*, 1995: 22–33.
37. Hayward, M., 2017: 16–17.
38. Levey, S. M. 'References to Dress in the Earliest Account Book of Bess of Hardwick', in *Costume*, vol.34, issue 1, January 2000: 20–2.
39. Nevinson, J. L. 'New Year's Gifts to Queen Elizabeth I, 1584', in *Costume*, vol.9, issue 1, January 1975: 27–31.
40. Hayward, M. 'The "Empresse of Flowers": The Significance of Floral Imagery in Two Portraits of Elizabeth I at Jesus College, Oxford', in *Costume*, vol.44, issue 1, June 2010: 20–7.
41. Reynolds, A. *In Fine Style: The Art of Tudor and Stuart Fashion*, Royal Collection Trust, 2013: 202.
42. Carter, A. J. 'Mary Tudor's Wardrobe', in *Costume*, vol.18, issue 1, April 2017: 9.
43. Reynolds, A., 2013: 204.
44. Donnell, S. *Feminizing the Enemy: Imperial Spain, Transvestite Drama, and the Crisis of Masculinity*, Bucknell University Press, 2002: 154.
45. Harvey, J. *Men in Black*, Reaktion Books, 1995: 72.
46. Reynolds, A., 2013: 28.
47. Benhamou, R. 'The Restraint of Excessive Apparel: England 1337–1604', in *Dress*, vol.15, issue 1, 1989: 29.
48. Act 2, scene 1.
49. Byrde, P. *The Male Image: Men's Fashion in England, 1300–1970*, Batsford, 1979: 115;

Newark, T. *Brassey's Book of Uniforms*, Brassey's Ltd, 1998: 37.

50. Defoe, D. *Memoirs of a Cavalier*, Cambridge University Press, 1809: 108.

51. Brooke, I. *Dress and Undress: The Restoration and Eighteenth Century*, Methuen Publishing, 1958: 23.

52. Newark, T., 1998: 35.

53. *Revolution in Fashion 1715–1815*, Kyoto Costume Institute, 1989: 151.

54. Currie, E. 'Prescribing Fashion: Dress, Politics and Gender in Sixteenth-Century Italian Conduct Literature', in *Fashion Theory*, vol.4, issue 2, 2000: 170.

55. Tiramani, J. 'Janet Arnold and the Globe Wardrobe: Handmade Clothes for Shakespeare's Actors', in *Costume*, vol.34, issue 1, 2000: 121.

56. Downing, S. J. *Fashion in the Time of William Shakespeare*, Shire Publications, 2014: 48.

57. 'A Parisian Correspondent', in *La Belle Assemblée: or Bell's Court and Fashionable Magazine*, London, May 1830: 209.

58. 'Costume of Paris', in *La Belle Assemblée: or Bell's Court and Fashionable Magazine*, London, September 1831: 120.

59. 'Records of the Beau Monde', in *La Belle Assemblée: or Bell's Court and Fashionable Magazine*, London, May 1831: 230.

60. 'Fashion in the France of Henry IV and Marie de' Medici', in *American Vogue*, 1 October 1922: 96.

61. Heywood, L. M. *Njinga of Angola: Africa's Warrior Queen*, Harvard University Press, 2017: 62.

62. *Ibid.*: 224, 229–30, 239.

63. Olsen, K. *Chronology of Women's History*, Greenwood Publishing Group, 1994: 71.

64. Heywood, L. M. 'The Angolan-Afro-Brazilian Cultural Connections', in *Slavery & Abolition*, vol.20, issue 1, 1999: 9–23; Fromont, C. 'Dancing for the King of Congo from Early Modern Central Africa to Slavery-Era Brazil', in *Colonial Latin American Review*, vol.22, issue 2, 2013: 184–208.

65. Burnard, J. *Chintz and Cotton: India's Textile Gift to the World*, Kangaroo Press, 1994: 50.

66. Crill, R. *Chintz: Indian Textiles for the West*, Victoria and Albert Museum, 2008: 14–15.

67. Hayward, M. 'Dressing Charles II: The King's Clothing Choices (1660–85)', in Coquery, N. and Pareysys, I. (eds.) *Se vêtir à la cour en Europe (1400–1815)*, Villeneuve d'Ascq, Centre de recherche du château de Versailles, Institut de recherches historiques du Septentrion et CEGES université de Lille, 2011.

68. Strong, R. 'Charles I's Clothes for the Years 1633 to 1635', in *Costume*, vol.1, issue 1, 1980: 73–89.

69. Mansel, P. *Dressed to Rule: Royal and Court Costume from Louis XIV to Elizabeth II*, Yale University Press, 2005: 50.

70. Many writers have focused on queer readings of Queen Christina and her subsequent representations; see, for example, Feinberg, L. 'Transgender Liberation: A Movement Whose Time Has Come', in Stryker, S. and Whittle, S. (eds.) *The Transgender Studies Reader*, Routledge, 2006: 214; and Gaines, J. 'The queen Christina tie-ups: Convergence of show

window and screen', in *Quarterly Review of Film and Video*, vol.11, issue 1, 1989: 35–60.

71. Stolpe, S. *Christina of Sweden*, Burns & Oates, 1966: 178; Buckley, V. *Christina Queen of Sweden: The Restless Life of a European Eccentric*, Harper Perennial, 2005.

72. Henri de Guise quoted in Popp, N. A. 'Expressions of power: Queen Christina of Sweden and patronage in Baroque Europe', Doctor of Philosophy (Ph.D) thesis, University of Iowa, 2015: 288–9.

73. Stadin, K. 'The masculine image of a great power', in *Scandinavian Journal of History*, vol.30, issue 1, 2005: 61–82; Pollock, G. 'Productive Illegibility: Gender, Monarchy and Self-Creation in the Histories, Images and Fictions of Queen Christina Vasa of Sweden', in Flicker, E. and Seidle, M. (eds.) *Fashionable Queens: Body – Power – Gender*, Peter Lang, 2014: 114–15.

74. 'Dresses: R. H. Macy & Co. Presents Clothes Inspired By Costumes Worn In "Queen Christina"', in *Women's Wear Daily*, 28 December 1933: 12.

75. 'The Queen Christina Look', photographed by Franco Rubartelli, American *Vogue*, 15 August 1968: 68–83.

76. Breward, C. *Fashion*, Oxford University Press, 2003: 24.

77. Mansel, P. *Dressed to Rule: Royal and Court Costume from Louis XIV to Elizabeth II*, Yale University Press, 2005: 8.

78. Calahan, A. and Trivette Cannell, K. (eds.) *Fashion Plates: 150 Years of Style*, Yale University Press, 2015: 2.

79. Lady Mary Wortley Montagu in Scarce, J. M. *Women's Costume of the Near and Middle East*, Routledge, 2014: 62.

80. *Ibid.*: 65.

81. For more, see Tuttle, D. M. 'Lady Mary Wortley Montagu as Critic of Feminine Cultural Constraints in the Turkish Embassy Letters', in *The Explicator*, vol.75, issue 1, 2017: 3–5.

82. Boer, I. 'Just a Fashion?: Cultural Cross-dressing and the Dynamics of Cross-cultural Representations', in *Fashion Theory*, vol.6, issue 4, 2015: 426–30; 'Turquerie', in *The Metropolitan Museum of Art Bulletin*, vol.26, no.5, January 1968: 233.

83. Breskin, I. '"On the Periphery of a Greater World": John Singleton Copley's "Turquerie" Portraits', in *Winterthur Portfolio*, vol.36, no.2/3, Summer/Autumn, 2001: 97–123.

Late Modern

1. Steele, V. and Major, J. S. (eds.) *China Chic: East Meets West*, Yale University Press, 1999: 29.

2. Spence, J. 'Portrait of an Emperor – Qianlong: Ruler, Connoisseur, and Scholar', in *ICON*, winter 2003/2004.

3. Yong, Y. 'Imperial Dress in the Qing Dynasty', in Wilson, M. with the Palace Museum Beijing, (eds.) *Imperial Chinese Robes From the Forbidden City*, Victoria and Albert Museum, 2010: 15.

4. Steele, V. and Major, J. S. (eds.), 1999: 18.

5. Anderson, A. *A Narrative of the British Embassy to China, in the Years 1792, 1793, and 1794: Containing the Various Circumstances of the Embassy, with Accounts of Customs and Manners of the

Chinese; And a description of the Country, Towns, Cities, &C, &C*, J. Debrett, 1795: 262.

6. Johnson, J. H. *Venice Incognito: Masks in the Serene Republic*, University of California Press, 2011: 12–13, 16.

7. *Ibid.*: 5, 42–4.

8. Kelly, I. *Casanova*, Hodder & Stoughton, 2009: 17.

9. Ruane, C. 'Subjects into Citizens: The Politics of Clothing in Imperial Russia', in Parkins, W. (ed.) *Fashioning the Body Politic: Dress, Gender, Citizenship*, Berg, 2002: 50.

10. Ruane, C. *The Empire's New Clothes: A History of the Russian Fashion Industry, 1700–1917*, Yale University Press, 2009: 23.

11. Matyjaszkiewicz, K. 'The Russian Costumes in Perspective', in *Russian Style 1700–1920: Court and Country Dress from the Hermitage*, Barbican Editions, 1987: 80.

12. Ruane, C., 2009: 152.

13. Yefimova, L. V., Aleshina, T. S. *Russian Elegance: Country and City Fashion*, Vivays Publishing, 2011: 9, 42, 104.

14. Matyjaszkiewicz, K., 1987: 77.

15. Chrisman-Campbell, K. *Fashion Victims: Dress at the Court of Louis XVI and Marie-Antoinette*, Yale University Press, 2015: 25–6.

16. Ribeiro, A. *Dress in Eighteenth-Century Europe, 1715–1789*, Yale University Press, 2002: 27.

17. For more on this, see Weber, C. *Queen of Fashion: What Marie Antoinette Wore to the Revolution*, Henry Holt & Co., 2006.

18. Kanai, J. I. 'One More Desire: Fashion Leaders of a Dramatic Era', in Handy, A. (ed.) *Revolution in Fashion: European Clothing 1715–1815*, Kyoto Costume Institute, 1989. 122.

19. Greig, H. *The Beau Monde*, Oxford University Press, 2013: 168.

20. Foreman, A. *Georgiana, Duchess of Devonshire*, HarperCollins UK, 1999: 37–8.

21. Greig, H. *The Beau Monde* Oxford University Press, 2013: 214.

22. *Ibid.*: 121.

23. 'The Large Hat', American *Vogue*, 1 March 1923: 132.

24. Wrigley, R. *The Politics of Appearances*, Berg, 2002: 187.

25. For more on the liberty cap, see Ribeiro, A. *Fashion in the French Revolution*, Batsford, 1988: 82–6.

26. Wrigley, R., 2002: 202.

27. *Ibid.*: 224.

28. *Ibid.*: 203.

29. Ribeiro, A., 1988: 119.

30. See, for example, Trevor-Roper, H. 'The Highland Tradition of Scotland', in Hobsbawn, E. and Ranger, T. (eds.) *The Invention of Tradition*, Cambridge University Press, 2013 [1983]; and Pittock, M. 'Plaiding the Invention of Scotland', in Brown, I. (ed.) *From Tartan to Tartanry: Scottish Culture, History and Myth*, Edinburgh University Press, 2010.

31. Trevor-Roper, H., 2013: 30–1.

32. Riach, A. 'Tartanry and its Discontents: The Idea of Popular Scottishness', in Brown, I. (ed.), 2010.

33. Pittock, M. in Brown, I. (ed.), 2010: 44; Thorburn, W. A. 'Military Origins of Scottish National Dress', in *Costume*, vol.10, issue 1, January 1976.

34. For more on this, see Kurokawa, Y. 'Vivienne Westwood's "Seditionaries" Clothes

and the Change in Japanese Girls' Cute Fashions in the Early 1990s', in *Costume*, vol.47, issue 1, July 2013: 63–78; and 'Tartan: Its Journey Through the African Diaspora', a project and exhibition by the Costume Institute of the African Diaspora: ciad.org.uk/past-events/tartan-its-journey-through-the-african-diaspora/.

35. Kelly, I. *Beau Brummell: The Ultimate Dandy*, Hodder & Stoughton, 2005: 185.

36. Jesse, W. *A Life of George Bryan Brummell, Esq.* (1844), in Kelly, I., 2005: 163.

37. Breward, C. 'Masculine Pleasures: Metropolitan Identities and the Commercial Sites of Dandyism, 1790–1840', in Reilly, A. and Cosbey, S. (eds.) *Men's Fashion Reader*, Fairchild Books, 2008: 69.

38. Inglis, F. *A Short History of Celebrity*, Princeton University Press, 2010: 63.

39. Mozer, H. J. '"Ozymandias," or De Casibus Lord Byron: Literary Celebrity on the Rocks', in *European Romantic Review*, vol.21, issue 6, 2010: 735; Winch, A. '"Drinking a Dish of Tea with Sapho": The Sexual Fantasies of Lady Mary Wortley Montagu and Lord Byron', in *Women's Writing*, vol.20, issue 1, 2013: 94.

40. Kelly, I., 2005: 166.

41. Langley Moore, D. 'Byronic Dress: A lecture given at the National Portrait Gallery, 11 October, 1969', in *Costume*, no.5, June 1971: 1.

42. Kelly, I., 2005: 165.

43. Langley Moore, D. in *Costume*, June 1971: 6–7.

44. For more on the discovery, see *Ibid.*

45. Bloomer, D. C. *Life and Writings of Amelia Bloomer*, Arena Publishing Company, 1895: 68.

46. Petrov, J. '"A Strong-Minded American Lady": Bloomerism in Texts and Images, 1851', in *Fashion Theory*, vol.20, issue 4, 2016: 397; Mullenix, E. R. 'Private Women/Public Acts: Petticoat Government and the Performance of Resistance', in *TDR*, vol.46, no.1, Spring 2002: 111.

47. Zakim, M. 'Sartorial Ideologies: From Homespun to Ready-Made', in *The American Historical Review*, vol.106, no.5, December 2001: 1582.

48. Fischer, G. V. '"Pantalets" and "Turkish Trowsers": Designing Freedom in the Mid-Nineteenth-Century United States', in *Feminist Studies*, vol.23, no.1, Spring 1997: 135.

49. Bloomer, D. C., 1895: 70.

50. Welters, L. 'Ethnicity in Greek Dress', in Eicher, J. B. (ed.) *Dress and Ethnicity: Change Across Space and Time*, Berg, 1999: 59–61.

51. Macha-Bizoumi, N. 'Amalia Dress: The Invention of a New Costume Tradition in the Service of Greek National Identity', in *Catwalk: The Journal of Fashion, Beauty and Style*, vol.1, no.1, 2012: 69–70.

52. Field, R. *Garibaldi*, Bloomsbury Publishing, 2012: 6.

53. Honeck, M. 'Garibaldi's Shirt: Fashion and the Making and Unmaking of Revolutionary Bodies', in Lerg, C. A. and Tóth, H. (eds.) *Transatlantic Revolutionary Cultures, 1789–1861*, Brill, 2017: 153.

54. 'The Fashions', in *The Englishwoman's Domestic Magazine*, December 1861: 93.

55. Honeck, M. in Lerg, C. A. and Tóth, H. (eds.), 2017: 158.

56. 'Waists', in *Women's Wear Daily*, 12 May 1911: 5; and 'Shirtwaist' *Women's Wear Daily*, 12 September 1952: 7.

57. For example, E. G. 'Fashion: The Allied French Colors', in *American Vogue*, 1 September 1915: 54; 'Costumes', in *Women's Wear Daily*, 14 May 1915: 25; 'Color In Paris', in *Women's Wear Daily*, 23 July 1915: 25.

58. Marx, K. *Capital: A Critique of Political Economy – The Process of Capitalist Production*, Cosimo, Inc., 2007: 51.

59. Lemire, B. 'Shifting Currency: The Culture and Economy of the Second Hand Trade in England, c.1600–1850', in Clark, H. and Palmer, A. (eds.) *Old Clothes, New Looks: Second Hand Fashion*, Berg, 2005: 34.

60. Stallybrass, P. 'Marx's Coat', in Spyer, P. (ed.) *Border Fetishisms: Material Objects in Unstable Spaces*, Routledge, 1998: 188.

61. For more on this, see Sullivan, A. 'Karl Marx: Fashion and Capitalism', in Rocamora, A. and Smelik, A. (eds.) *Thinking Through Fashion: A Guide to Key Theorists*, I. B. Tauris, 2015.

62. *Punch* magazine in Dolan, T. 'The Empress's New Clothes: Fashion and Politics in Second Empire France', in *Woman's Art Journal*, vol.15, no.1, Spring/Summer, 1994: 23.

63. Gormally, M. F. 'The House of Worth: Portrait of an Archive', in *Fashion Theory*, vol.21, issue 1, 2017: 111.

64. Dolan, T. 'Skirting the Issue: Manet's Portrait of *Baudelaire's Mistress, Reclining*', in *The Art Bulletin*, vol.79, issue 4, 1997: 624.

65. *Ibid.*: 627.

66. See, for example, Miller, E. C. 'Sustainable Socialism: William Morris on Waste', in *The Journal of Modern Craft*, vol.4, issue 1, 2011: 7–25.

67. Garfield, S. *Mauve: How One Man Invented a Colour that Changed the World*, Faber and Faber, 2000.

68. Morris, W. 'Dyeing as an Art', in *The Decorator and Furnisher*, vol.19, no.6, March 1892: 217–18.

69. Wilson, E. *Bohemians: The Glamorous Outcasts*, Tauris Parke Paperbacks, 2003: 173.

70. Solomon-Godeau, A. 'The Legs of the Countess', in *October*, vol.39, Winter, 1986: 69.

71. Demange, X. 'A Nineteenth-century Photo-novel', in Apraxine, P. and Demange, X. *La Divine Comtesse: Photographs of the Countess de Castiglione*, Metropolitan Museum of Art and Yale University Press, 2000: 54–72.

72. Fox, R. 'A Disconcerting Pact with Gravity: Nineteenth-century Acrobats and the Failure of Transcendence', in *Nineteenth-Century Contexts*, vol.38, issue 2, 2016: 82.

73. *Mémoires de Léotard*, Deuxième Édition, 1860: 173.

74. 'The Leotard Idea', in *Harper's Bazaar*, January 1943: 35.

75. See, for example, 'The Climate of Summer: The Seaside Leotard and the Swimming Tutu', in *Harper's Bazaar*, May 1954: 79–91.

76. Harder, K. B. 'Leotards and "Tightsomania"', in *American Speech*, vol.35, no.2, May 1960: 104.

77. 'Vogue's Eye View: The Leotard Boom', in *American Vogue*, 1 November 1943: 93.

78. Fuchs, E., Kasahara, T. and Saaler, S. (eds.) *A New Modern History of East Asia*, V&R Unipress, 2017: 119–20.

79. Cho, S. 'The Ideology of Korean Women's Headdresses during the Chosŏn Dynasty', in *Fashion Theory*, vol.21, issue 5, 2017: 553–71; Yi Sŏng-mi 'Women in Korean History and Art', in Roberts, C. and Dong-hwa, H. (eds.) *Rapt in Colour: Korean Textiles and Costumes of the Chosŏn Dynasty*, Powerhouse Museum and the Museum of Korean Embroidery, 1998: 25–7.

80. Kumja Paik Kim 'Profusion of Colour: Korean Costumes and Wrapping Cloths of the Choson Dynasty', in Roberts, C. and Dong-hwa, H., 1998: 10.

81. Key-Soak Geum and DeLong, M. R. 'Korean Traditional Dress as an Expression of Heritage', in *Dress*, vol.19, issue 1, 1992: 61.

82. Nelson, S. M. 'Bound Hair and Confucianism in Korea', in Hiltebeitel, A. and Miller, B. D. (eds.) *Hair: Its Power and Meaning in Asian Cultures*, State University of New York Press, 1998: 108, 111.

83. Yung-Chung Kim, Ihwa Yŏja Taehakkyo, Han'guk Yŏsŏng Sa P'yŏnch'an Wiwŏnhoe *Women of Korea: A History from Ancient Times to 1945*, Ewha Womans University Press, 1979: 215.

84. Steele, V. (ed.) *A Queer History of Fashion: From the Closet to the Catwalk*, Yale University Press and the Fashion Institute of Technology, 2013: 20.

85. Adburgham, A. *Liberty's: A Biography of a Shop*, Allen & Unwin, 1975: 31.

86. Reid, F. *Keir Hardie: The Making of a Socialist*, Croom Helm, 1978: 141.

87. Morris, M. 'The Most Respectable Looking of Revolutionaries', in *Cultural and Social History*, vol.12, issue 3, 2015: 324–5.

88. *Ibid.*: 325.

89. Holman, B. *Keir Hardie*, Lion Books, 2012: 66.

90. Engels, F. *The Condition of the Working Class in England*, in Stallybrass, P. 'Marx's Coat', in Spyer, P. (ed.) *Border Fetishisms: Material Objects in Unstable Spaces*, Routledge, 1998: 193.

91. Frost, W. and Laing, J. *Imagining the American West Through Film and Tourism*, Routledge, 2015: 184.

92. Riley, G. *The Life and Legacy of Annie Oakley*, University of Oklahoma Press, 2012: 21–2, 141–2.

93. Nottage, J. H. 'Fashioning the West: The Pre-Twentieth-Century Origins of Western Wear', in George-Warren, H. and Freedman, M. (eds.) *How the West was Worn: A History of Western Wear*, Abrams, 2001: 18.

94. For more, see Wilson, L. 'American Cowboy Dress: Function to Fashion', in *Dress*, vol.28, issue 1, 2001: 40–52.

95. 'Annie Oakley "Goes Gunning"—In Jersey Prints by Renoir', in *Women's Wear Daily*, 26 April 1946: 29.

96. 'Western Fashions to Launch Annie Oakley Program in May: Three-Piecers', in *Women's Wear Daily*, 26 March 1952: 44.

97. Powles de Frece, M. A. *Recollections of Vesta Tilley*, Hutchinson, 1934: 25.

98. 'As Seen by Him', in *American Vogue*, 14 June 1894: 266.

99. 'As Seen by Him', in *American Vogue*, 16 May 1895: 312–13.

100. Powles de Frece, M. A., 1934: 195.

101. *Seattle Post-Intelligencer*, in Berg, S. C.

'Sada Yacco in London and Paris, 1900: Le Rêve Réalisé', in *Dance Chronicle*, vol.18, issue 3, 1995: 344; 'Theater: Japanese Plays', in *American Vogue*, 8 March 1900: 3.
102. Berg, S. C. *Dance Chronicle*, 1995: 343–4, 396.
103. For more, see Molony, B. 'Gender, Citizenship, and Dress in Modernizing Japan', in Roces, M. and Edwards, L. (eds.) *The Politics of Dress in Asia and the Americas*, Sussex Academic Press, 2007: 81–100.
104. Dalby, L. *Kimono: Fashioning Culture*, University of Washington Press, 2001: 65–6, 91; Kennedy, A. *Japanese Costume: History and Tradition*, Adam Biro, 1990: 34.
105. Lady Colin Campbell, art critic for *The World*, 13 June 1900: 13–14, in Berg, S. C. *Dance Chronicle*, 1995: 359.
106. For more, see Rado, M. M. 'The Hybrid Orient: Japonisme and Nationalism of the Takashimaya Mandarin Robes', in *Fashion Theory*, vol.19, issue 5, 2015: 583–616; Yamaguchi, A. 'Kimonos for Foreigners: Orientalism in Kimonos Made for the Western Market, 1900–1920', in *The Journal of Dress History*, vol.1, issue 2, Autumn 2017.
107. Dalby, L., 2001: 81, 91–2, 338, 341–2.
108. For more on this, see Leblon, B. *Gypsies and Flamenco: The Emergence of the Art of Flamenco in Andalusia*, University of Hertfordshire Press, 1995: 63–5; Goldberg, K. M. 'Sonidos Negros: On the Blackness of Flamenco', in *Dance Chronicle*, vol.37, issue 1, 2014: 85–113; Papenbrok, M. 'History of Flamenco', in Schreiner, C. (ed.) *Flamenco: Gypsy Dance and Music from Andalusia*, Amadeus Press, 2000 [1985]: 39.
109. Leblon, B., 1995: 43, 47.
110. Schreiner, C. (ed.), 2000 [1985]: 98; Leblon, B., 1995: 96.
111. Leblon, B., 1995: 95.
112. Quote from 1893 in Worth, S. 'Andalusian Dress and the Andalusian Image of Spain: 1759–1936', submitted for the Doctor of Philosophy, Ohio State University, 1990: 128.
113. *Ibid.*: 20–1, 146.
114. *Ibid.*: 22, 113.
115. For more on this, see Strasdin, K. *Inside the Royal Wardrobe: A Dress History of Queen Alexandra*, Bloomsbury Academic, 2017.
116. 'Royal "Peasants" in the Forest of Sinaia'/'Fete Days with Prince and Peasant', in *American Vogue*, 18 September 1909: 368–70, 432.
117. Davis, M. E. *Ballets Russes Style: Diaghilev's Dancers and Paris Fashion*, Reaktion Books, 2010: 65–6.
118. Vassiliev, A. *Beauty in Exile: The Artists, Models, and Nobility who Fled the Russian Revolution and Influenced the World of Fashion*, Harry N. Abrams, 2000: 181.
119. Vettese, S. 'The Ballets Russes Connection with Fashion', *Costume*, vol.42, issue 1, June 2008: 139.
120. 'A Royal Marriage of World-Wide Interest', in *American Vogue*, 15 September 1922: 75.
121. See Bartlett, D. 'Glitz and Restraint – Paris Haute Couture on Display', in *Fashion Theory*, vol.18, issue 4, 2014: 427–46; and Lloyd, C. F. 'Liberty's Embroidery Workrooms: Memories of working there during the years 1918 to 1924', in *Costume*, vol.10, issue 1, January 1976: 86–90.

122. Lady Susan Townley, 'London! Brilliant, Eccentric, Whimsical: A Review', in *Arts & Decoration*, vols.21-2, 1924: 46.
123. 'The Wardrobe of Her Majesty Queen Marie of Roumania', in *American Vogue*, 15 August 1924: 39; 'A Queen Makes Her Choice', in *American Vogue*, 15 November 1926: 174.
124. 'Roumania, the Colourful', in American *Vogue*, 15 March 1928: 194, 196.

20th & 21st Centuries

1. Jullian, P. 'People Are Talking About: Extravagant Casati', in American *Vogue*, 1 September 1970: 424.
2. Baron de Meyer 'The Substance of a Venetian Dream', in *American Vogue*, 15 February 1916: 108.
3. Ryersson, S. D. and Yaccarino, M. O. *Infinite Variety: The Life and Legend of the Marchesa Casati*, University of Minnesota Press, 2004: 43.
4. *Ibid.*: 57
5. Kaplan, J. H. and Stowell, S. *Theatre and Fashion: Oscar Wilde to the Suffragettes*, Cambridge University Press, 1994: 152.
6. Parkins, W. '"The Epidemic of Purple, White and Green": Fashion and the Suffragette Movement in Britain 1908–14', in Parkins, W. (ed.) *Fashioning the Body Politic*, Berg, 2002: 102.
7. *Ibid.*: 97.
8. Kaplan, J. H. and Stowell, S., 1994: 173.
9. Chapman, J. 'The Argument of the Broken Pane', in *Media History*, vol.21, issue 3, 2015: 238.
10. White, R. '"You'll Be the Death of Me": Mata Hari and the Myth of the *Femme Fatale*', in Hanson, H. and O'Rawe, C. (eds.) *The Femme Fatale: Images, Histories, Contexts*, Palgrave Macmillan, 2010: 75.
11. Bentley, T. *Sisters of Salome*, Yale University Press, 2002: 101.
12. Hubbard, L. 'As Danced Before Buddha', in American *Vogue*, 15 December 1913: 98.
13. LaValley, S. 'Hollywood and Seventh Avenue: The Impact of Period Films on Fashion', in Maeder, E. (ed.) *Hollywood & History: Costume Design in Film*, Thames & Hudson/Los Angeles County Museum of Art, 1987: 36.
14. 'Does Hollywood Create?', in American *Vogue*, 1 February 1933: 60.
15. 'Cardin returns with Mata Hari', in *Women's Wear Daily*, 11 April 1962: 4-5.
16. 'What's Going On: The Thirteenth Biennial Convention...The General Federation of Women's Clubs', in *Harper's Bazaar*, July 1916: 35.
17. Schmidt, C. and Tay, J. 'Undressing Kellerman, Uncovering Broadhurst: The Modern Woman and "Un-Australia"', in *Fashion Theory*, vol.13, issue 4, 2009: 484.
18. See, for example, Lucas, J. 'Making A Statement: Annette Kellerman Advances the Worlds of Swimming, Diving and Entertainment', in *Sporting Traditions*, vol.14, no.2 (May 1998), 25–35.
19. 'Annette Kellerman Sullivan, 87, "Million Dollar Mermaid"', *The New York Times* obituary, 6 November 1975: nytimes.com/1975/11/06/archives/annette-kellerman-sullivan-87-million-dollar-mermaid-dead-played-55.html.

20. For more on Kellerman's films, see Chapman, D. 'Amazons, Vampires and Daredevils: Athletic Women in Silent Films', in *The International Journal of the History of Sport*, vol.31, issue 13, 2014: 1577–97.
21. *Ibid.*: 1587.
22. 'Paris Closes and Opens a Season', in *American Vogue*, 15 August 1912: 21.
23. For more, see Davis, M. E. *Ballets Russes Style: Diaghilev's Dancers and Paris Fashion*, Reaktion Books, 2010; Bartlett, D. 'Léon Bakst and Fashion: Beyond and After the Ballets Russes', in *Costume*, vol.51, issue 2, 2017: 210–34; Vettese, S. 'The Ballets Russes Connection with Fashion', in *Costume*, vol.42, issue 1, 2008.
24. Ryersson, S. D. and Yaccarino, M. O. *Infinite Variety: The Life and Legend of the Marchesa Casati*, University of Minnesota Press, 2004: 40.
25. Romola Nijinsky in Nadelhoffer, H. *Cartier*, Chronicle Books, 2007: 335.
26. Yaeger, L. 'Rites of Spring: Erdem Pays Homage to the Ballets Russes', *Vogue.com*, September 23rd, 2010: vogue.com/article/rites-of-spring-erdem-pays-homage-to-ballet-russes.
27. Moholy-Nagy, L., Molnár, F. and Schlemmer, O. *The Theater of the Bauhaus*, Wesleyan University Press, 1961: 25.
28. See also Koss, J. 'Bauhaus Theater of Human Dolls', in *The Art Bulletin*, vol.85, no.4, December 2003: 724–45.
29. Introduction by Walter Gropius in Moholy-Nagy, L., Molnár, F. and Schlemmer, O., 1961: 9.
30. 'We Like the Way He Looks', in American *Vogue*, 1 September 1949: 194–5.
31. Beaton, C. 'Wedding of the Duke and Duchess of Windsor', in *American Vogue*, 1 July 1937: 32–5.
32. 'H.R.H. Started It', in *American Vogue*, 15 January 1934: 36–7, 72, 74; 'Prince Of Wales Wears Fair Island Sweater At Golf Tournament', in *Women's Wear Daily*, 23 October 1922: 18; and 'Knit Notes From The Shops: Amerino Shirts—A Cotton And Wool Mixture', in *Women's Wear Daily* supplement, 28 April 1933: 11.
33. Dawson, E. '"Comfort and Freedom": The Duke of Windsor's Wardrobe', *Costume*, vol.47, issue 2, 2013: 208.
34. 'A Weekend with H.R.H. the Duke and the Duchess of Windsor', in *American Vogue*, 15 November 1967: 98-103.
35. Sebba, A. *That Woman: The Life of Wallis Simpson, Duchess of Windsor*, Phoenix, 2011: 215-17, 225–6.
36. Timmer, P. 'Sonia Delaunay: Fashion and Fabric Designer', in McQuaid, M. and Brown, S. (eds.) *Colour Moves: Art and Fashion by Sonia Delaunay*, Thames & Hudson, 2011: 25.
37. Slevin, T. 'Sonia Delaunay's *Robe Simultanée*: Modernity, Fashion, and Transmediality', in *Fashion Theory*, vol.17, issue 1, 2013: 31.
38. Timmer, P. in *Colour Moves: Art and Fashion by Sonia Delaunay*, 2011: 28–44.
39. 'The Riviera Season', in *Harper's Bazaar*, April 1916: 122.
40. Warner, P. C. 'Public and Private: Men's Influence on American Women's Dress for

Sport and Physical Education', *Dress*, vol.14, issue 1, 1988: 51.
41. 'World-Famous Players on the Courts of Nice', in American *Vogue*, 15 April 1926: 114.
42. 'Suzanne Lenglen Shows how to Dress for Tennis', in American *Vogue*, 1 December 1926: 64–5.
43. 'Sport and Country: Cotton or Linen', in *Harper's Bazaar*, April 1932: 70.
44. Stewart, M. L. *Dressing Modern French-women: Marketing Haute Couture, 1919–1939*, Johns Hopkins University Press, 2008: 209.
45. Skillen, F. '"It's possible to play the game marvellously and at the same time look pretty and be perfectly fit": Sport, Women and Fashion in Interwar Britain', *Costume*, vol.46, issue 2, 2012: 176.
46. Wagg, S. 'Sacred turf: the Wimbledon tennis championships and the changing politics of Englishness', in *Sport in Society*, vol.20, issue 3, 2017: 403.
47. For a full discussion, see Dellamora, R. *Radclyffe Hall: A Life in the Writing*, University of Pennsylvania Press, 2011.
48. Glick, E. *Materializing Queer Desire: Oscar Wilde to Andy Warhol*, State University of New York Press, 2009: 68.
49. Wilson, E. 'What Does a Lesbian Look Like?', in Steele, V. (ed.) *A Queer History of Fashion: From the Closet to the Catwalk*, Yale University Press and the Fashion Institute of Technology New York, 2013: 175.
50. *Newcastle Daily Journal and North Star*, in Doan, L. *Fashioning Sapphism: The Origins of a Modern English Lesbian Culture*, Columbia University Press, 2001: 111.
51. Garber, M. *Vested Interests: Cross-Dressing and Cultural Anxiety*, Routledge, 1992: 155.
52. Doan, L., 2001: 112.
53. Marcketti, S. B. and Angstman, E. T. 'The Trend for Mannish Suits in the 1930s', in *Dress*, vol.39, issue 2, 2013: 139–52.
54. See 'First Lady of the Sky—Some High-Flown Fashions', in American *Vogue*, 15 January 1933: 30–1, 66; and 'Made for Motion', in American *Vogue*, 1 June 1934: 90.
55. Jay, K. 'No Bumps, No Excrescences: Amelia Earhart's Failed Flight into Fashions', in Benstock, S. and Ferriss, S. (eds.) *On Fashion*, Rutgers University Press, 1994: 77.
56. Staszak, J-F. 'Performing race and gender: the exoticization of Josephine Baker and Anna May Wong', in *Gender, Place & Culture*, vol.22, no.5, 2015: 638.
57. See Metzger, S. 'Patterns of Resistance?: Anna May Wong and the Fabrication of China in American Cinema of the Late 30s', in *Quarterly Review of Film and Video*, vol.23, no.1, January 2006: 1–11; and Leong, K. J. *The China Mystique: Pearl S. Buck, Anna May Wong, Mayling Soong, and the Transformation of American Orientalism*, University of California Press, 2005.
58. *Harper's Bazaar*, November 1935: 55.
59. Hodges, G. R. *Anna May Wong: From Laundryman's Daughter to Hollywood Legend*, Hong Kong University Press, 2012: 209.
60. Johnson, R. 'Need Some Met Gala Inspiration? Look No Further Than Anna May Wong', in American *Vogue*, 1 May 2015: vogue.com/article/met-gala-fashion-inspiration-anna-may-wong.
61. See, for example, Henderson, M. G.

'Josephine Baker and *La Revue Negre*: from ethnography to performance', in *Text and Performance Quarterly*, vol.23, issue 2, 2003: 107–33.
62. Baker, J. C. and Chase, C. *Josephine Baker: The Hungry Heart*, Cooper Square Press, 2001: 120; Wood, E. *The Josephine Baker Story*, Sanctuary Publishing, 2000: 88, 137.
63. 'Jo Baker's fabulous wardrobe', in *Ebony*, July 1964: 4, 105.
64. 'Hosiery: Style Importance Of Burnt Foliage Tones Cited For Early Fall: Creole Shade Named "Josephine Baker" For Charleston Dancer In Paris "Folies Bergere"', in *Women's Wear Daily*, 2 July 1926: 26.
65. Dryansky, G. Y. 'Baker's back again', in *Women's Wear Daily*, 28 December 1973: 12.
66. Jules-Rosette, B. *Josephine Baker in Art and Life: The Icon and the Image*, University of Illinois Press, 2007: 135, 145.
67. *Ibid*.: 146.
68. Struensee, C. 'Josephine Baker Promotion Stirs Up Windows At Macy's', in *Women's Wear Daily*, 12 March 1991: 27.
69. For more, see Tarlo, E. *Clothing Matters: Dress and Identity in India*, C. Hurst & Co. Publishers, 1996: 70–87.
70. Chakrabarty, D. 'Clothing the Political Man: A reading of the use of khadi/white in Indian public life', in *Postcolonial Studies*, vol.4, issue 1, 2001: 28.
71. Gandhi, M. K. *Khadi: Hand-Spun Cloth, Why and How*, Navajivan Publishing House, 1959: 11.
72. See, for example, 'The Spirit Is Youth, the Style Is Money', in *The New York Times*, 6 January 1969; '"Meditation Look:" A Radical Change', in *Los Angeles Times*, 8 April 1968, cited in Kutulas, J. 'Dedicated followers of fashion: peacock fashion and the roots of the new American man, 1960–70', in *The Sixties: A Journal of History, Politics and Culture*, vol.5, issue 2, 2012: 167–84.
73. Frazier, G. 'The Peacock Revolution', in *Esquire*, vol.70, 1968: 212.
74. Rose, B. 'Vogue's Spotlight: Art', in American *Vogue*, 1 April 1969: 152.
75. McCarthy, P. 'An Original', in *Women's Wear Daily*, 25 September 1979: 6.
76. Dearborn, M. V. *Mistress of Modernism: The Life of Peggy Guggenheim*, Houghton Mifflin Harcourt, 2004: 41–2.
77. McCarthy, P. in *Women's Wear Daily*, 1979: 6.
78. Rose, B. in American *Vogue*, 1969: 152.
79. Aragón, A. F. 'Uninhabited Dresses: Frida Kahlo, from Icon of Mexico to Fashion Muse', in *Fashion Theory*, vol.18, issue 4, 2014: 543.
80. Cordry, D. and Codry, D. *Mexican Indian Costumes*, University of Texas Press, 1968: 273–80; Block, R. and Hoffman-Jeep, L. 'Fashioning National Identity: Frida Kahlo in "Gringolandia"', in *Woman's Art Journal*, vol.19, no.2, Autumn/Winter 1998–9: 12.
81. Block, R. and Hoffman-Jeep, L. in *Woman's Art Journal*: 11.
82. Wolfe, B. D. 'Rise of Another Rivera', in American *Vogue*, 1 November 1938: 131.
83. For more, see Aragón, A. F. in *Fashion Theory*, vol.18, issue 4, 2014: 543.
84. McNeil, P. '"Why Don't You"—Think for Yourself? Diana Vreeland after Diana Vreeland', in *Fashion Theory*, vol.18, issue 4, 2014: 421.

85. *Ibid*.: 419; Weymouth, L. 'Vreelandmania', in Immordino Vreeland, L. *Diana Vreeland: The Eye Has to Travel*, Harry N. Abrams, 2011: 19.
86. Rossi-Camus, J. 'DV: An Edited Chronology', in Clark, J. and Frisa, M. L. (eds.) *Diana Vreeland after Diana Vreeland* Marsilio Editori, 2012: 213.
87. Talley, A. L. 'Vreeland's Show', *The New York Times*, 6 December 1981: nytimes. com/1981/12/06/magazine/fashion-vreeland-s-show.html. For an overview of the arguments surrounding Vreeland's curatorial approach, see Steele, V. 'Museum Quality: The Rise of the Fashion Exhibition', in *Fashion Theory*, vol.12, issue 1, 2008: 7–30.
88. For more, see De la Haye, A. 'Vogue and the V&A Vitrine', in *Fashion Theory*, vol.10, issues 1–2, 2006: 127–52; and Palmer, A. 'Untouchable: Creating Desire and Knowledge in Museum Costume and Textile Exhibitions', in *Fashion Theory* vol.12, issue 1, 2008: 31–63.
89. Nodell, A. 'Remembering JFK's "Effortless" Style 100 Years After His Birth', in *Women's Wear Daily*, 29 May 2017: wwd.com/ eye/lifestyle/remembering-jfk-style-100-birthday-10896511/.
90. See, for example, Shaw, M. 'The Kennedys: a Private View at Hyannis Port', in American *Vogue*, 1 July 1961: 50–7.
91. 'Sportswear And Separates: Ivy Look Continues', in *Women's Wear Daily*, 7 March 1957: 12.
92. Zakim, M. 'Customizing the Industrial Revolution: The Reinvention of Tailoring in the Nineteenth Century', in *Winterthur Portfolio*, vol.33, no.1, Spring, 1998: 41–58.
93. Winick, C. 'Fan mail to Liberace', in *Journal of Broadcasting*, vol.6, issue 2, 1962: 130–1.
94. Colker, D. 'Michael Travis dies at 86; costume designer for Liberace', in *Los Angeles Times*, 3 May 2014: latimes.com/local/ obituaries/la-me-michael-travis-20140504-story.html.
95. Clemente, D. and O'Connor, A. 'Why Liberace's Costumes Mattered', in *The Atlantic*, 6 June 2013: theatlantic.com/ entertainment/archive/2013/06/why-liberaces-costumes-mattered/276568/.
96. Bergman (1993) in Udy, D. 'Diva Las Vegas: queering space in the entertainment capital of the world', in *Gender, Place & Culture: A Journal of Feminist Geography*, vol.24, issue 3, 2017: 369.
97. For more on the trial, see Glen, P. '"Oh You Pretty Thing!": How David Bowie "Unlocked Everybody's Inner Queen" in spite of the music press', in *Contemporary British History*, vol.31, issue 3, 2017: 407–29; Bengry, J. 'Profit (f)or the Public Good?', in *Media History*, vol.20, issue 2, 2014: 146–66.
98. Michals, D. 'Furs: Lippin Signs Pact To Make A Licensed Liberace Line', in *Women's Wear Daily*, 11 November 1986: 12.
99. Mackenzie, M. *Dream Suits: The Wonderful World of Nudie Cohn*, Lannoo Publishers, 2012: 100.
100. Liberace, *The Wonderful Private World of Liberace*, Turner Publishing Company, 2003: 222.
101. Bruzzi, S. *Undressing Cinema: Clothing and Identity in the Movies*, Routledge, 1997: 7.

102. Murphy, B. (ed.) *Critical Insights: A Streetcar Named Desire by Tennessee Williams*, Salem Press, 2010: 36.
103. 'Interview with Elia Kazan', in Knopf, R. (ed.) *Theater and Film* Yale University Press, 2005: 349.
104. Strauss, T. 'The Brilliant Brat', in *LIFE*, 31 July 1950: 49–52.
105. 'Meet the Champs', in *Photoplay*, October 1953: 40–3, 102, in Cohan, S. *Masked Men: Masculinity and the Movies in the Fifties*, Indiana University Press, 1997: 242.
106. Crowther, B. *The New York Times* movie review, 31 December 1953: nytimes.com/movie/review?res=9B03E7DC123EE53BB-C4950DFB4678388649EDE.
107. Tulloch, C. *The Birth of Cool: Style Narratives of the African Diaspora*, Bloomsbury Publishing, 2016: 132–3.
108. *The Autobiography of Malcolm X*, 1966: 127, cited in Tulloch, 2016: 133.
109. See, for example, Peiss, K. *Zoot Suit: The Enigmatic Career of an Extreme Style*, University of Pennsylvania Press, 2011.
110. See, for example, Cosgrove, S. 'The Zoot Suit and Style Warfare', in McRobbie, A. (ed.) *Zoot Suits and Second-Hand Dresses*, Macmillan, 1989; Alvarez, L. *The Power of the Zoot: Youth Culture and Resistance During World War II*, University of California Press, 2009.
111. Tulloch, C. *The Birth of Cool: Style Narratives of the African Diaspora*, Bloomsbury Publishing, 2016. 135.
112. Cartier-Bresson, H. 'An Island of Pleasure Gone Adrift', in *LIFE*, 15 March 1963: 42.
113. 'Communists: The Cult of Che', in *TIME*, vol.91, no.20, 17 May 1968.
114. Edwards, L. H. *Johnny Cash and the Paradox of American Identity*, Indiana University Press, 2009: 53.
115. Frook, J. 'Hard-Times King of Song', in *LIFE*, 21 November 1969: 48.
116. Edwards, L. H, 2009: 53.
117. For more, see Mackenzie, M., 2012.
118. Harvey, J. *Men in Black*, Reaktion Books, 1995: 26–7.
119. Ford, T. C. *Liberated Threads: Black Women, Style, and the Global Politics of Soul*, University of North Carolina Press, 2015: 15.
120. See, for example, Klemsrud, J. 'Her Hairdo Started the "Afro" Trend', in *The New York Times*, 8 October 1966: 38.
121. 'Life Guide', in *LIFE*, 14 December 1962: 12.
122. For more, see Ford, T. C., 2015: 13–27.
123. Fleming, T. 'A Marriage of Inconvenience: Miriam Makeba's Relationship with Stokely Carmichael and her Music Career in the United States', in *Safundi*, vol.17, no.3, May 2016: 312–38.
124. Olowu, D. 'Life in Style', *Frieze*, 28 August 2016: frieze.com/article/life-style.
125. Breward, C. *Fashioning London: Clothing and the Modern Metropolis*, Berg, 2004: 175.
126. 'Vogue's Own Boutique', in American *Vogue*, 1 May 1966: 232–4.
127. Hunt, M. *Real Life*, Flamingo HarperCollins, 1995 [1986]: 89.
128. For more on this, see Mercer, K. 'Black Hair/Style Politics', in *New Formations* 3, Winter 1987: 33–54; and Ford, T. C., 2015: 104–8.
129. Hunt, M., 1995 [1986]: 104.

130. 'Beauty Bulletin: The Natural', in American *Vogue*, 1 January 1969: 134.
131. Garland, P. 'Sounds', in *Ebony*, January 1973: 29.
132. See Durosomo, D. 'Fela Kuti, The Radical Fashion Icon', *Okay Africa*, 25 September 2017: okayafrica.com/fela-kuti-radical-fashion-icon/.
133. Tchouaffe, O. J. 'Fela Ransome-Kuti: Black Icons and Issues of Representation', in Falola, T. and Genova, A. (eds.) *Yoruba Creativity: Fiction, Language, Life and Songs*, Africa World Press, 2005: 315–16; Tenaille, F. *Music is the Weapon of the Future: Fifty Years of African Popular Music*, Chicago Review Press, 2002: 74.
134. Bidouzo-Coudray, J. 'Buki Akib | Crafting At The Core Of Luxury', *Another Africa*, 18 July 2012: anotherafrica.net/brand/buki-akib-crafting-at-the-core-of-luxury.
135. 'Inspired By Fela Anikulapo Kuti! Lifestyle Brand, Kancky Debuts Its Resort '16 "Road To Kalakuta" Collection', *OnoBello*, 23 July 2016: onobello.com/inspired-by-fela-anikulapo-kuti-lifestyle-brand-kancky-debuts-its-resort-16-road-to-kalakuta-collection/.
136. '10 Fab Things That Inspire Solange Knowles', *Glamour*, 14 May 2012: glamour.com/story/solange-knowles-what-inspires.
137. Alexander, E. 'Bowie Crowned Most Stylish Briton In History', *Vogue*, 15 October 2013: vogue.co.uk/article/david-bowie-is-britons-best-dressed-in-history.
138. Gorman, P. 'Bowie and Fashion', *SHOWstudio*, 24 March 2016: showstudio.com/project/david_bowie_oooh_fashion/essay_paul_gorman.
139. *Harper's & Queen*, July 1971.
140. Mower, S. 'Fashion takes a BOWIE', in *Harper's & Queen*, May 1993: 144.
141. *Ibid.*; Gorman, P., 2016.
142. Dalby, L., 2001: 86.
143. Thian, H. M. 'Moss Garden: David Bowie and Japonism in Fashion in the 1970s', in Devereux, E., Dillane, A. and Power, M. (eds.) *David Bowie: Critical Perspectives*, Routledge, 2015: 128–46.
144. 'Kansai Is Out To Win The War Of Tokyo Fashion: His Fashion Empire Is Expanding', in *Women's Wear Daily*, 25 March 1981: 24.
145. Gondola, D. 'Dream and Drama: The Search for Elegance among Congolese Youth', in *African Studies Review*, vol.42, no.1, April 1999: 26.
146. Newell, S. 'Circuitously Parisian: Sapeur Parakinship and the Affective Circuitry of Congolese Style', in Cole, J. and Groes, C. (eds.) *Affective Circuits: African Migrations to Europe and the Pursuit of Social Regeneration*, University of Chicago Press, 2016: 292.
147. For more on Paris, see Friedman, J. 'The Political Economy of Elegance: An African Cult of Beauty', in Friedman, J. (ed.) *Consumption and Identity*, Routledge, 1995; and Gondola, D. in *African Studies Review*, April 1999: 28–32.
148. Martin, P. 'Contesting Clothes in Colonial Brazzaville', in *The Journal of African History*, vol.35, issue 3, 1994: 401–26.
149. Thomas, D. 'Fashion Matters: La Sape and Vestimentary Codes in Transnational Contexts and Urban Diasporas', in *MLN*,

vol.118, no.4, September 2003: 958; Hoenig, K. H. and Nyirahuku, B. 'Inserting Bana Molokai Popular Culture Texts into the Rwandan English Literature Classroom', in *English Studies in Africa*, vol.49, issue 1, 2006: 47–69.
150. Howarth, D. 'Postmodern Design: Grace Jones' Maternity Dress by Jean-Paul Goude', *Dezeen*, 11 September 2015: dezeen.com/2015/09/11/postmodernism-fashion-design-grace-jones-maternity-dress-jean-paul-goude/.
151. Gruen, J. *Keith Haring: The Authorized Biography*, Prentice Hall, 1992: 116.
152. Jones, G. and Morley, P. *I'll Never Write My Memoirs*, Simon & Schuster, 2015: 131–6.
153. See Thrasher, S. W. 'Prince broke all the rules about what black American men should be', in the *Guardian*, 22 April 2016: theguardian.com/music/2016/apr/21/prince-broke-expectations-black-american-men-musical-genius-performances; and Arceneaux, M. 'How Prince Helped Me Define My Black Masculinity and Love Myself', in *Teen Vogue*, 22 April 2016: teenvogue.com/story/prince-masculinity-self-love.
154. Poussaint, A. F. 'An Analytical Look at the Prince Phenomenon', part of Norment, L. 'Prince: What is the Secret of his Amazing Success?', in *Ebony*, June 1985: 166–70.
155. Adducci, S. and Karsen, S. '"Purple Rain" Exclusive: The Stories and the Sketches Behind the Movie's Groundbreaking Style', in *Billboard*, 28 April 2016: billboard.com/articles/news/magazine-feature/7348550/purple-rain-style-stories-sketches-exclusive-interview.
156. Sanneh, K. 'Harlem Chic', in *The New Yorker*, 25 March 2013: newyorker.com/magazine/2013/03/25/harlem-chic.
157. *Ibid.*; Romero, E. *Free Stylin': How Hip Hop Changed the Fashion Industry*, Praeger, 2012: 85.
158. Sanneh, K., 2013.
159. Brown, E. 'Uptown Legend', in *Interview*, 24 June 2015: interviewmagazine.com/culture/dapper-dan-of-harlem#slideshow_477914.
160. Mower, S. 'Resort 2018: Gucci', *Vogue*, 29 May 2017: vogue.com/fashion-shows/resort-2018/gucci.
161. Cochrane, L. 'Gucci to collaborate with bootlegger Dapper Dan', the *Guardian*, 11 September 2017: theguardian.com/fashion/2017/sep/11/gucci-to-collaborate-with-bootlegger-dapper-dan.
162. Winfrey, O. 'Oprah Talks to RuPaul About Life, Liberty and the Pursuit of Fabulous', 16 January 2017: oprah.com/inspiration/oprah-talks-to-rupaul#ixzz56qgBmkuv.
163. Wortham, J. 'Is "RuPaul's Drag Race" the Most Radical Show on TV?', *The New York Times*, 24 January 2018: nytimes.com/2018/01/24/magazine/is-rupauls-drag-race-the-most-radical-show-on-tv.html.
164. Biography, Yinka Shonibare MBE: yinkashonibarembe.com/biography/.
165. Sylvanus, N. *Patterns in Circulation: Cloth, Gender, and Materiality in West Africa*, University of Chicago Press, 2016; Dogbe, E. 'Unraveled Yarns: Dress, Consumption, and Women's Bodies in Ghanaian Culture', in *Fashion Theory*, vol.7, issues 3–4, 2003: 377–95.

166. See Miller, M. L. *Slaves to Fashion: Black Dandyism and the Styling of Black Diasporic Identity*, Duke University Press, 2009.
167. See Rice, A. 'Tracing Slavery and Abolition's Routes and Viewing Inside the Invisible: The Monumental Landscape and the African Atlantic', in *Atlantic Studies*, vol.8, issue 2, 2011: 253–74.
168. Rys, D. 'Beyoncé's *Lemonade* Highest-Selling Album Globally in 2016; Drake Lands Top Song: IFPI', in *Billboard*, 25 April, 2017: billboard.com/articles/columns/hip-hop/7775037/ifpi-beyonce-lemonade-highest-selling-album-2016-drake-song.
169. Arzumanova, I. 'The Culture Industry and Beyoncé's Proprietary Blackness', in *Celebrity Studies*, vol.7, issue 3, 2016: 421–4; Brooks, D. A. 'How #BlackLivesMatter Started a Musical Revolution', in the *Guardian*, 13 March 2016: theguardian.com/us-news/2016/mar/13/black-lives-matter-beyonce-kendrick-lamar-protest; Edgar, A. N. and Toone, A '"She Invited Other People to that Space": Audience Habitus, Place, and Social Justice in Beyoncé's *Lemonade*', in *Feminist Media Studies*, 2017.
170. hooks, b. 'Moving Beyond Pain', 9 May 2016: bellhooksinstitute.com/blog/2016/5/9/moving-beyond-pain; Hopkins, S. 'Girl Power-Dressing: Fashion, Feminism and Neoliberalism with Beckham, Beyoncé and Trump', in *Celebrity Studies*, 2017; London, D. 'Beyoncé's Capitalism, Masquerading as Radical Change', in *Death and Taxes*, 9 February 2016: deathandtaxesmag.com/280129/beyonce-capitalism-black-activism/.
171. Carlos, M. 'Meet the Stylist Behind *That* Beyoncé Throwback Gucci "Formation" Video Look', in *Vogue*, 8 February 2016: vogue.com/article/super-bowl-beyonce-gucci-alessandro-michele-formation-music-video-stylist; McColgin, C. 'Beyoncé's Stylist B. Akerlund on Finding the Perfect Yellow Dress for "Lemonade"', *Hollywood Reporter*, 25 April 2016: www.hollywoodreporter.com/news/beyonces-lemonade-stylist-yellow-roberto-887455.
172. 'Beyoncé and Tina Knowles on Fashion Collection and Pregnancy', *CNN*, 20 September 2011: edition.cnn.com/2011/09/19/showbiz/beyonce-tina-knowles/index.html.
173. Koda, H. 'Introduction', in Boman, E. *Rare Bird of Fashion: The Irreverent Iris Apfel*, Thames & Hudson, 2007: 9.
174. Sheffield, L. 'Iris Apfel Is Now a Wearable Tech Designer', in *Harper's Bazaar*, 14 January 2016: harpersbazaar.com/fashion/designers/a13702/iris-apfel-wearable-tech-line/.
175. Boman, E., 2007: 34.
176. *Ibid.*
177. Abnett, K. *Business of Fashion*, 28 July 2016: businessoffashion.com/articles/intelligence/styling-politicians-donald-trump-theresa-may-hillary-clinton.
178. For more, see Albright, M. *Read My Pins: Stories from a Diplomat's Jewel Box*, HarperCollins, 2009.
179. For more on this, see Lauret. M. 'How to read Michelle Obama', in *Patterns of Prejudice*, vol.45, issues 1–2, 2011: 95–117.
180. Foley, B. 'A Woman of Substance',

in *Women's Wear Daily*, 20 January 2009: 1, 4–6.
181. 'Fashion Awards Honor Michelle Obama', CBS, 16 June 2009: www.cbsnews.com/news/fashion-awards-honor-michelle-obama/.
182. Foreman, K. 'Michelle Boosts European Designers', *Women's Wear Daily*, 6 April 2009: 2; Cartner-Morley, J. and Chilvers, S. 'Michelle Obama does London – the fashion story so far', in the *Guardian*, 2 April 2009: theguardian.com/world/2009/apr/02/michelle-obama-fashion.
183. Talley, A. L. 'Power of Change: Leading Lady', in American *Vogue*, 1 March 2009: 428–35, 504, photographed by Annie Leibovitz. See also, Mortensen, T. 'Visually Assessing the First Lady in a Digital Age: A Study of Michelle Obama as Portrayed by Journalists and the White House', in *Journal of Women, Politics & Policy*, vol.36, issue 1, 2015: 43–67.
184. Kusama in Applin, J. *Yayoi Kusama: Infinity Mirror Room – Phalli's Field*, The MIT Press, 2012: 8.
185. Matsui, M. 'Yayoi Kusama', in *Index*, 1998: indexmagazine.com/interviews/yayoi_kusama.shtml.
186. For more, see Judah, H. 'Inside an Artist Collaboration', in *Business of Fashion*, 4 December 2013: businessoffashion.com/articles/intelligence/inside-an-artist-collaboration.
187. Swanson, C. 'Exclusive: Yayoi Kusama Talks Louis Vuitton, Plus a First Look at the Collection', in *The Cut*, 9 July 2012: thecut.com/2012/07/exclusive-yayoi-kusama-talks-louis-vuitton.html.
188. Adichie, C. N. *We Should All Be Feminists*, Fourth Estate, 2014.
189. McHenry, J. 'Chimamanda Ngozi Adichie Doesn't Think Beyoncé's Feminism Is Flawless: "Her Style Is Not My Style"', in *The Cut*, 7 October 2016: thecut.com/2016/10/adichies-feminism-isnt-beyoncs-feminism.html.
190. Cartner-Morley, J. 'Maria Grazia Chiuri on Fashion, Feminism and Dior: "You Must Fight for Your Ideas"', in the *Guardian*, 18 March 2017: theguardian.com/fashion/2017/mar/18/maria-grazia-chiuri-fashion-feminism-fight-for-ideas.
191. Topping, A. 'Chanel's Karl Lagerfeld cheered and jeered for "feminist" fashion statement', in the *Guardian*, 30 September 2014: theguardian.com/fashion/2014/sep/30/chanel-karl-lagerfeld-cheered-jeered-feminist-staement-fashion-catwalk.
192. Okwodu, J. 'The Women's March Pussyhat Takes Milan Fashion Week', *Vogue*, 25 February 2017: vogue.com/article/milan-fashion-week-ready-to-wear-fall-2017-missoni-pussyhats.
193. Adichie, C. N. 'My Fashion Nationalism', in *Financial Times*, 20 October 2017: ft.com/content/03c63f66-af6b-11e7-8076-0a4bdda92ca2.
194. Friedman, V. 'On Election Day, the Hillary Clinton White Suit Effect', in *The New York Times*, 7 November 2016: nytimes.com/2016/11/07/fashion/hillary-clinton-suffragists-white-clothing.html.
195. Clinton, H. R. *What Happened*, Simon & Schuster, 2017: 88.

196. *Ibid.*
197. Ballgowns, shoulder pads and scrunchies, to name a few: Garber, M. 'Why the Pantsuit?', in *The Atlantic*, 2 August 2016: theatlantic.com/entertainment/archive/2016/08/youre-fashionable-enough-hillary/493877/.
198. Ellis, K. 'Fashion Industry Contributions Favor Clinton', in *Women's Wear Daily*, 31 October 2016: wwd.com/business-news/government-trade/fashion-favors-hillary-clinton-10691202/; Yotka, S. 'Marc Jacobs, Tory Burch, and Public School Design Campaign Tees for Hillary Clinton', *Vogue.com*, 18 February 2016: vogue.com/article/hillary-clinton-made-for-history-fashion-designer-t-shirts.
199. Abnett, K. 'Styling Politicians in the Age of Image Wars', in *Business of Fashion*, 28 July 2016: businessoffashion.com/articles/intelligence/styling-politicians-donald-trump-theresa-may-hillary-clinton.
200. Clinton, H. R., 2017: 88.
201. Douglas, A. 'Point Of View: The Extraordinary Hillary Clinton', in American *Vogue*, 1 December 1998: 231–9.
202. Clinton, H. R., 2017: 256.
203. Friedman, V. 'On Election Day, the Hillary Clinton White Suit Effect', in *The New York Times*, 7 November 2016: nytimes.com/2016/11/07/fashion/hillary-clinton-suffragists-white-clothing.html; Harwood, E. 'Hillary Clinton Wears Symbolic White to Donald Trump's Inauguration', in *Vanity Fair*, 20 January 2017: vanityfair.com/style/2017/01/hillary-clinton-white-ralph-lauren-suit-inauguration.
204. For example, speaking on the 150th anniversary of Elizabeth Cady Stanton's 'Declaration of Sentiments', as covered in Douglas, A. 'Point Of View: The Extraordinary Hillary Clinton', in American *Vogue*, 1 December 1998: 231–9.
205. Kaplan, J. H. and Stowell, S., 1994: 173.
206. Sauers, J. 'Why Model Halima Aden Refuses to Remove Her Hijab for Fashion', in *Harper's Bazaar*, 6 November 2017: harpersbazaar.com/culture/features/a13127587/halima-aden-hijab-model/.
207. For more on this, see Lewis, R. *Muslim Fashion*, Duke University Press, 2015; and Janmohamed, S. *Generation M: Young Muslims Changing the World*, I. B. Tauris, 2016.
208. Sauers, J. *Harper's Bazaar*, 6 November 2017.
209. Fox, C. 'Muslim Model Halima Aden on Faith and Facing Opposition', in *Financial Times*, 3 November 2017: ft.com/content/19666aec-bd91-11e7-9836-b25f8adaa111.
210. Khalaf, R. 'High Fashion and Hijabs are Good for Business', in *Financial Times*, 3 March 2017: www.ft.com/content/a5de6502-0283-11e7-aa5b-6bb07f5c8e12.
211. Friedman, V. 'Women, Fashion Has You Covered', in *The New York Times*, 6 April 2017: nytimes.com/2017/04/06/fashion/covered-up-fashion-style-of-the-decade.html; Cartner-Morley, J. 'The Great Cover Up: Why We're All Dressing Modestly Now', in the *Guardian*, 13 September 2017: theguardian.com/fashion/2017/sep/13/the-great-cover-up-why-were-all-dressing-modestly-now.

Index

Page numbers in *italics* refer to illustrations

Acknowledgements

Huge thanks to scholars Hilary Davidson and Mairi MacKenzie for their notes and suggestions on Eleanor of Aquitaine and Johnny Cash respectively. A big thank you to the Octopus team for providing invaluable support, feedback and patience: Joe Cottington, Pauline Bache, Giulia Hetherington and Yasia Williams–Leedham, as well as Carrie Kania. As ever, heartfelt thanks to Dana, Rachael, mum, John, Toby and Rob Flowers.

Picture credits